EMPATH SURVIVAL GUIDE AND THE SECRETS OF THE ENNEAGRAM

2-in-1 Book

Discover The 9 Personality Types, Who You Really Are and How to Make Emotional Awareness Your Best Quality

EMPATH SURVIVAL GUIDE: HOW TO MAKE YOUR PERSONALITY A SUPERPOWER

Embrace The Gift of Empathy, Learn How to Protect Yourself From Narcissistic Relationships and Welcome Your Happiest Self

Table of Contents

Introduction 7

Chapter One - Are You an Empath? 11
What is an Empath? 11
10 Signs You're An Empath 12
Empathic, Introverted and Sensitive: What is the Difference? 15
8 Misconceptions About Empaths 17

Chapter Two - Understanding the Empath Gift 20
The Science Behind Empathy and Empaths 21

Chapter Three - The Empath Reality 34
5 Bad Habits that Empaths Must Let Go 36
The 5 Common Health Problems of Empaths 37

Chapter Four - The Injured Empath 41
What is Compassion Fatigue? 43
Signs of an Injured Empath 46
Beware: The Victim Complex 48
The Truth About Empaths and Addiction 50

Chapter Five - The Dangers of Being an Empath 53
Why Narcissists Are Drawn to Empaths 56
Why Empaths are Drawn to Narcissists 57
Signs an Empath is with an Emotional Vampire 58

Chapter Six - Healing the Empath Heart 63
5 Healing Activities for Empaths to Relax 63
Powerful Techniques for Healing and Self-Protection 68
Positive Affirmations All Empaths Must Know 70

Chapter Seven - The Healthy, Happy Empath 72
The 5 Powerful Lessons Every Empath Must Learn 72
Daily Practices of a Healthy Empath 74
Stop Empathizing with Pain and Start Empathizing with Joy 77

Chapter Eight - Empathy as a Superpower 80
The 7 Natural Gifts that All Empaths Possess 80

The Best Jobs for Empaths 82
Conclusion **88**

Introduction

There is a unique breed of individuals who are gifted with the ability to not only experience their emotions and those of the people around them; they can also experience the physical pain of other people. These individuals walk into a room and within minutes, they can accurately pick on the vibes of the people in the room. This may sound like a cool superpower that belongs on the set of X-Men but in reality, it is something that can be very difficult to deal with and not many people are emotionally and mentally equipped to manage these gifts. You may identify such persons as people who are overly sensitive. Psychology experts profile them as empaths and their story is not always one of those happily ever after types.

For the longest time, emotions have been frowned on as a weakness and displaying them was described as a feminine trait at best. In worst-case scenarios, people who showed their emotions one too many times were regarded as persons who have no control over how they feel. Derogatory terms like "unpredictable", "walking eggshells", "cry baby" and so many other names that are not fit to print are used to tag people who dare to show their emotions. The general negative perception about emotions has woven itself into the very foundation of the society which is the family. There are a lot of families today who enforce strict measures to deter any display of emotions at home. This need to shut down a very crucial aspect of one's self has led many to suffer silently for a better part of their lives. For an empath, they live with the double trauma of dealing with their own emotions as well as the pain of others. This leaves them constantly emotionally overwhelmed. If you picked up this book, chances are you are an empath or you know an empath who struggles with their emotional burden.

But, what if I told you that those very emotions that you feel cripple you and your ability to thrive can be channeled into making you a better version of yourself and in so doing, you can enrich your life? Sounds too good to be true right? Well, here is one truth that many of us heard but don't really believe because they have been dumped in the same category as those ineffective life clichés people dish out. Your emotions are anything but weak. In fact, it is described as one of the most powerful forces possessed by humans and before we go any further in this book, I can tell you that shutting your emotions down is not going to do you any good. The only way forward is to embrace those feelings by choosing to accept your abilities as an empath.

Being an empath goes beyond understanding your emotions. As an empath, you embrace the emotions of others. The wealth of understanding you acquire in this process gifts you with a unique perspective of the world and the people that you encounter daily. This goes a long way to help you foster relationships that are more meaningful and impactful. Most importantly, as an empath, you develop a deeper connection with yourself that truly empowers you to understand pain. This is not some new-age psychobabble fad that is trending at the moment. This is you taking back the power from people who have tagged the way you truly feel as weak and evolving into the "real you" that you are meant to be.

With this book, you can finally take off the mask you have been forced to wear by the society and step into your reality. As an empath who had to navigate the process of my "becoming" without a guide, I know how difficult to make sense of how you feel. I spent lots of hours daily scouring through the internet for information on these rainbows of emotions that I go through every day. I have come close to several breakdowns not because I had a lot of bad experiences or that I was taking on more workload than I normally would. I was just constantly overwhelmed by what I was feeling. People would come to me with their problems because I had a knack for being such a great listener and I could connect with them in ways that they found comforting. However, I also ended up having to deal with the emotional aftermath of their predicaments. I sought counseling and for a while, that helped me. But, I still sought validation from the people I deal with on a day to day basis. I didn't want to crumble emotionally in front of them so that I could keep being their go-to counselor.

This meant I had to act like I had my life together 100% of the time even if in reality, it felt like I could barely keep the seams from falling apart. In very succinct terms, I was a mess. With the contents of this book, I was able to;

- Make sense of the emotions I was feeling
- Find the strength to embrace these seemingly chaotic parts of myself
- Learn to manage my emotions better
- Unlock my natural intuitive nature and pay more attention to my instincts
- Become better at managing my relationships with people

Maybe you are reading my story and feeling like you are looking into the mirror of your own life. Here is an assurance, if I can find my way back, so can you. However, there is a caveat. Living as an empath requires you being deliberate about your decisions. Anything less could send you on a downward spiral to a dark place that not many people recover from. Before you flip over to the next chapter, I want you to take a moment and decide right here, right now that you are going to be more deliberate about the choices that you make going forward.

That said, the information you would receive in this book are practical steps you can take daily to help you better manage your emotions while navigating the murky emotional waters of other people. At the end of this book, you should be able to stand on a rooftop and proudly declare that you know who you are. That knowledge is powerful and very uplifting. So, to begin the next chapter of your life, turn over to the next page. Things are about to get exciting.

Chapter One - Are You an Empath?

I was a teenager when I had my first encounter with the word "empath." It was from a television series that was popular at the time. In this series, the empath was portrayed as someone who was gifted with divine powers and the ability to feel everything the people around them felt. This empath could feel their pain, their joy, their anger, and even their fears. In this fictional world, the powers of the empath were transferable but if anyone other than a true empath attempted to take these powers, they would be crushed by the weight of the emotions they were forced to experience. This interpretation of an empath is certainly fascinating but it is also very extreme.

Sci-fi lovers share a similar view with the creators of this fantasy series. Culturally, empaths are believed to be humans who possess this paranormal ability to accurately sense the emotional state of others. A popular empath in today's sci-fi trend would be Mantis from the movie, *Guardians of the Galaxy*. Again, this is all very cool but reality tells us a different story.

What is an Empath?

An empath is simply a person with a heightened awareness of the emotions around them. Beyond this awareness, empaths tend to show a lot of empathy towards other people – so much they can experience the emotions of others as if they were their own. Empaths don't just observe people; they have the innate ability to experience them from the inside. The term "ability" is used loosely here. It does not connote the existence of supernatural traits, rather it is directed at a personality trait that uniquely defines them.

In psychology, empaths are described as people who have a great amount of empathy for others. Given everything I've explained so far, it might feel a little disappointing to see empaths defined with such simplicity. Empaths are powerfully unique because they can sense emotions that the people around them try to hide. Without the right information, however, this "uniqueness" can cause a lot of frustration. That said, how can you tell if you are truly an empath and not simply projecting what you hope you are?

I have compiled a list that explores the characteristics of most empaths. If you relate to six or more of the following traits, you are likely an empath.

10 Signs You're An Empath

1. Crowded spaces cause you to feel overwhelmed

When you are in a sea of people, their emotions wash over you like waves and for a person who has a tendency to feel everything, it can leave you feeling overwhelmed. The sensation is akin to experiencing sensory overload where all of your senses are firing off in different directions.

2. You personalize the experiences of others

When a friend comes to you with stories that have strong emotional content, you don't just listen and try to gauge their current state of mind. You see yourself walking in their shoes and reliving their experiences as if they happened to you. At the end of that conversation, you are not just an observer but an active participator in the event. This leaves you just as emotionally riled up as the person who shared their experience with you.

3. You are labeled as "emotional" or "too sensitive"

The way people describe you can give a little insight into your personality. Again, it is not often accurate but it speaks to the actions carried out by you that lead to the general perception of you as any being either too emotional or too sensitive. Now being emotional goes beyond the ability to cry at the drop of the hat. It infers that you get riled up easily.

4. Dealing with people leaves you feeling exhausted

There are people who go through an entire rainbow of emotions in a matter of minutes and these kinds of people can be exhausting to deal with even for the regular person. For an empath, it is twice as bad. You might speak with the mildest mannered person and still get exhausted. Why? Because you can sense the genuine emotions underneath the polite façade. Empaths have a strong radar for someone's true feelings, and they are rarely fooled by pretenses.

5. Most people feel understood by you

This one is a no brainer because you actually understand people. Your ability to see things from their perspective and empathize with them gives you a unique connection to them. In a weird but commendable way, you have this "you are them" bond that puts you in their shoes. For this reason, people tend to be drawn to you. They may feel seen in ways they don't normally feel seen. Sadly, not many people understand empaths, except for other empaths.

6. You are mostly an introvert

Your need to deal with people in very limited doses puts you on the outside of social events, but you likely don't mind it that much. You may even take pleasure in it. Empaths are more likely to be introverted because absorbing the emotions of others can get exhausting, so they tend to need a lot of alone time. Extroverted empaths do exist, but they are rare.

7. You can intuitively sense emotions

This is a big indicator that you are an empath. You are hardly ever fooled by the exterior charms and smiling façade. And if a person makes the mistake of coming to you with lies, you can detect it in a heartbeat without even having to ask questions. There is no technique to this when it comes to you. You are not looking out for that elevated pulse, dilated pupils, or sweaty palms. An empath just knows.

8. You feel connected to nature

This is another general human trait. It is not definitive but it is very common with empaths. Your connection to nature goes beyond the love of trees and sounds of chirping birds. These things give you pleasure but they also give you a sense of rejuvenation. Some people feel replenished after a good night's rest, some seek solace in food but for you, nature is what gets your juices up and flowing.

9. You can never say no to a person in need

Your experiences of other people's pain, suffering or joy does not end with you "feeling" what they feel. It compels you to act. You are not going to leave that little girl crying in the corner simply because her mom is there with her. You want to help make her feel better. Dropping a few coins in the cup for that homeless man is not going to cut it for you. You go home, grab a nice pair of socks, a warm and lovingly used blanket and hand it to him. And if that man stops coming to the area, you might be one of the first to notice. Because empaths have a hard time saying no, many of them struggle with taking on more than they can handle. They want to help everyone, and this can leave them feeling drained.

10. You can empathize with nearly everyone

It's not just about feeling the emotions of homeless people and crying children. Let's face it, it's easy to empathize with the vulnerable people in our society, and any kind person would. Empaths can feel empathy for basically everyone. If two people get in a fight, an empath may not agree with the actions of the aggressor, but they can still have empathy for them. They are able to pinpoint the feelings that caused the person to behave that way and they can empathize with that deep need. A true sign of an empath is when they can emotionally connect with someone that everyone else has turned away from.

Before you started this book, you likely already suspected you were an empath. Now that you've affirmed this, how does it feel? I remember how relieved I felt to finally discover the concept of an empath. It can be a liberating experience to finally identify with something, and to know you're not alone.

Now, let's clear up something important. There are a few words that are used interchangeably with the word "empath.' They may have been used to describe certain aspects of an empath but they do not in any way mean that a person who possesses these qualities is an empath. It is important to provide a clear distinction so as to avoid confusion going forward.

Empathic, Introverted and Sensitive: What is the Difference?

Let us start with the standard dictionary definition of these words before we explore it in depth. A person who is described as empathic essentially shows the ability to understand and share the feelings of another person. An introvert, on the other hand, is a shy and reclusive person who feels more energized when they spend time with themselves. And finally, a sensitive person is someone who is quick to react to the actions or reactions of others. As we can see, these are three different traits with three different meanings. While it is quite possible for a true empath to possess each of these three traits, none of these traits alone can make you an empath.

There are people who have the ability to empathize with others. They feel bad for the pain another person is going through but that does not make them all empaths. Empathy is a wonderful human trait that can give birth to kindness. Empaths, on the other hand, don't just feel bad about the pain of others, they personalize it and make it their own. It takes skillful discipline for an empath to get to a place where their interpretation of the pain of others does not cripple them emotionally.

Some empaths become introverted because they want to hide away from the distress that frequent interactions with people cause them. However, they need those interactions with people to fully make use of their empathic abilities. If they continue to hide away in solitude, that empathic nature may become buried and they'll simply become introverts. Now introverts actually derive pleasure in being alone. Beyond the basic necessity of human interaction (and even then, with very limited people), the introvert takes no pleasure in engaging with people outside of those they have a bond with. For empaths, this solitude is meant to provide a brief reprieve from the onslaught of emotions that hits them during social interactions.

Finally, being sensitive does not immediately translate to a hyper-awareness of the emotions of other people. In fact, in many cases, it can speak to a heightened awareness of only the self. Sensitive people can be acutely aware of their wants and needs, or at the very least, when they're not getting what they want and need. They have a fixed perception of what they feel is right or wrong and when words, actions or perceived reactions go against this information they have of themselves, they react. Even when they react to information affecting others, it is usually centered on their perception of the experiences of others. Many arrogant and narcissistic individuals can be accurately described as sensitive, and they are the opposite of an empath. Ever seen a narcissist get emotional because they aren't getting their way? Exactly. Many narcissists may even call themselves empaths as a way to excuse their inappropriate emotions, but never forget, a true empath must have empathy for other people.

In summary, these can be wonderful traits to have as a person and depending on your personality type, they can serve you well. However, there is more to being an empath than this. Generally speaking, the misuse of certain words to identify an empath are not the only misconceptions out there.

8 Misconceptions About Empaths

1. Empaths are weak

This is just one of the many derogatory labels used by people who do not understand the compassion of an empath. These people look down on any display of emotion other than anger. In reality, empaths can be some of the strongest people you'll ever meet. It can be exhausting to feel so many emotions so easily, and it takes true strength to rise again after feeling so overwhelmed.

2. Empaths cannot be leaders

An organization where there is no form of empathy in management would result in a toxic environment where workers cannot thrive, and they may eventually abandon their posts. An empathic leader is not constantly overflowing with emotions; an empathic leader can simply see his or her employees as human beings, and not just cogs in their machines. Leaders who can empathize with their employees will be more liked by those employees. And when workers in an organization have mutual respect for one another, that organization instantly becomes a fantastic team.

3. Empaths cannot be rational

I believe this is the biggest misconception of them all. An empath is someone who has more than just the facts when they conduct their analyses. Their ability to combine facts with the knowledge they draw from their emotional well gives them a more complete picture of the situation at hand. An empath is not bogged down by emotions in their decision-making, they simply have more information to act on. Empaths may take longer to make a decision, since they have more to consider, but empathy does not impede someone's sense of rationality.

4. Empaths are psychic

This is one of those myths that I wish we didn't have to dispel. Given the accuracy with which an empath can decipher true emotions and catch a liar mid-act, you have to wonder if there is some supernatural angle to it. There's nothing supernatural about it. Empaths are just very skilled at reading microexpressions, tone, and body language. They don't pick up these emotions out of nowhere, the signs are there all along; it's just that most people can't read them.

5. All empaths are introverts

The fact is, most empaths display some introverted tendencies but they are not always introverts. There are plenty of empaths who are extroverts, and many of them are better at hiding it when they feel emotionally overwhelmed. They still need time to recharge and reboot after social scenarios, but they feel more compelled to get back out there once they've had the rest they need.

6. Empaths are fictional characters made up by comic books

I want to launch into a litany of words to disprove this but the fact that you and I exist is enough to show this is not true. Psychologists have publicly acknowledged that empaths do exist and they can even identify what makes us the way we are. Do we need more evidence than that?

7. Empaths are always crying and over-emotional

Most people expect an empath to have an emotional meltdown every hour or so. Our abilities as empaths allow us to access a doorway that not many people can reach and sometimes, what we find on the other side can be very disconcerting and in some cases overwhelming. But, that image of the empath who is constantly in the fetal position crying their eyes out is completely inaccurate. While empaths *can* get very emotional, only a small percentage of empaths are in that state permanently. After a while, empaths learn to cope with their gift. They tend to be aware of when they need to withdraw to prevent themselves from getting to that state.

8. Empaths are victims of trauma

Many victims of trauma can turn out to be empaths, but it's never caused by the trauma itself. Sometimes empaths can live perfectly lucky and stable lives, without much exposure to trauma at all, and they'll still strongly empathize with those who are different from them. This is what makes empaths so incredible. Most people need to experience something to learn from it, but empaths can absorb it instantly.

Chapter Two - Understanding the Empath Gift

Given everything that you've felt in your lifetime, you may feel reluctant to regard empathic qualities or abilities as a gift. And who can blame you? Your emotional journey up to this point has been akin to a rollercoaster ride. Most people have difficulty processing the emotions that they encounter. An empath can go through a whole menu of emotions before the morning is over and that is not all. You experience these emotions at a level of intensity that would normally erode what I like to call your emotion nerve points (they are like the numbers on the scale except, in this case, they are not assessing your weight but your limits). Many people would be broken if they were to experience a fraction of what you feel. At this point, you and your emotions are like a mountain with an active volcano. Your exterior hides the turmoil going on inside.

You are probably thinking, "This part-time writer and full-time empath is doing a poor job of selling the idea of seeing your empathic abilities as a gift." Well, that's because everything I've outlined can indeed be considered a weakness, if looked at through the wrong lens. But do you want to know a secret? You can easily make this weakness your superpower. You just need to know how.

Your ability to process a variety of emotions faster than the average person takes a lot of strength. The way you experience emotions and interactions with so much depth is a new kind of intelligence. And to be the human equivalent of a volcano? Come on! How awesome is that?

Many people consider the empath gift as a superpower, but it can actually be explained with science. Let's get deeper, shall we?

The Science Behind Empathy and Empaths

The explanations I've given for empathy, until now, have come from a psychological and experiential point of view. But what does science have to say about it? A surprising amount of research has been done on the subject, and there are more than a handful of theories out there to explain the empath experience. Some of these theories are hogwash and would not hold their own in any science court. I found a few quite interesting.

I examined as many scientific theories as possible in the course of my research. I sorted them into different folders: the utterly crazy, the science-fiction and the ones that truly gave me pause. I'll share the best theories that made the most sense to me. And how about just one of the silly ones to end on a laugh?

Theory #1:

The guys who spend their careers studying the brain had to get a top spot on this list and they did not disappoint. According to them, empaths behave the way they do because of the mirror effect. The mirror effect essentially tells us that when we see someone do something, the part of our brains that is responsible for executing those same actions is triggered. Without our realization, that action is executed neurologically. And even though in reality, that action was never carried out by us, our brain relays the information to us as though we've truly performed those actions. Subsequently, we experience the consequences of those actions first-hand as if they happened to us.

Let's say your friend tells you about their horrible breakup and how she had to pack up all her ex-partner's things into a suitcase. An empathic person immediately puts themselves in that position. It's almost as if you were there yourself, packing away the belongings of the person you're about to say goodbye to forever. You weren't there, but it feels real to you. You feel the sadness in its entirety. The part of your brain that would be active during that scenario is, indeed, active now. And all you needed was to hear the story from your friend. That's the life of an empath.

I am willing to bet that you've experienced this before. According to neuroscientists, when we see a person take a certain action, our brain tells us we've done the same thing and we experience what they feel. Neurologically speaking, we have actually walked a mile in their shoes.

The focus of the study was on empathy and not empaths in particular. And what it proved is that empathy is a choice. Yes, you read that right. The brain's transmission of signals may have sounded like an involuntary reaction such as a blinking reflex, but actually, the brain decides in less than a nanosecond whether it's going to engage in the mirror effect. The display of empathy becomes a choice. Psychopaths adamantly refuse to participate in that process by deliberately detaching themselves emotionally.

This second study fine-tuned the purpose of their research. It was not just about empathy in this case now. It was meant to explain why some people are more empathetic than others. The person in charge of this project decided against using the word 'empath.' Instead, 'altruist' was used. It is important to note that there are different types of altruists. You have the kin-based altruist. As the name implies, these guys are very empathetic towards people they consider closely related to them. A mother who keenly experiences the anguish of her child displays empathy like no other but that does not really make her an empath now, does it? The second group of altruists is classified under the reciprocity-based group. They are what I like to call, the scratch my back and I scratch your back type of giver. For them, a favor is a bond that they hold in high esteem with every intention of paying it forward no matter the cost to them. You ever watch those movies where the hero calls on an 'old friend' who owes him a favor to help him or her complete a mission. More often than not, this old friend dies but not before telling the hero that they have paid their debt [so sad when that happens]. Well, that is what we are talking about here. And then you have the third group of guys who do what they do simply because they genuinely care about the welfare of the person that they are doing this good deed for. They do not have to have a prior relationship with the person and as a matter of fact, the people in this group prefer to do their generous giving anonymously. These non-cape wearing heroes are classified as care-based altruists in the experiment and they were the main focus in this research. That said, let us get back to the research.

The participants in this where people who had done selfless acts like donating an organ to a complete stranger and other really cool stuff [that might have you considering what your next 'giving' would be if you know what I mean]. They were paired with people who have never done that and both groups were asked to look at different images showing different emotional expressions. Their brains were mapped to monitor their reaction to these images and the results documented. What it showed was that the amygdalae which are the portion of the brain responsible for processing emotions among other things appeared to be 8 percent bigger than the regular non-altruist in the group which is incredible. Of course, they also examined the other guys at the other end [the psychopaths] and what they found was that the amygdalae of psychopaths were 18 percent smaller than average. Now, this made sense to me. The idea that empaths are essentially people with a neurological bonus in the right are. Who knew 8 percent could make that much of a difference, right? But this brain phenomenon was not the only thing that stood them apart. Other aspects of their lives were studied and it showed that they [the care-based altruists] were evidently more humble than their peers. This is why they reacted to the pain and fears of complete strangers as though it were their own. And this brings us to the point of this research. The research was guided by the role that fear plays in the decisions made by altruists. Let me break that down for you.

Empaths are more than just givers. The key thing for empaths is experiencing the emotions of others as though it were their own. There are no limits to the range of emotions that they feel. They can feel the rage of others, the pain, and even their joys. This experiment focused on the giving aspect of empathy and not just the experiential element which is crucial to the full definition of an empath. The researchers wanted to find out if there was a way to clearly identify true empaths. I would say that what this was able to successfully achieve was tell us that some people are visibly more sensitive to the distress of others and are more motivated to act on it because they have processed and personalized the experience of the person in distress [again, the mirror effect comes to play here] but it still doesn't fully address the issue. However, I am willing to take that 8 percent bigger amygdalae they discovered.

This final research took theory from the lab into what I can best describe as 'hooey' waters. But it does make sense. Especially since it is coming from a professor of psychology. The first research I discussed here focused on the mirror effect. This research focused on what they called the mirror-touch synesthesia. According to the article I read, this is a phenomenon where the line between what is actually experienced and what is witnessed is blurred. In other words, what you see and what you feel are almost the same thing. Now mirroring the pain of another person is a fairly common experience. As a guy, you see a guy getting punched in his nether region can inspire a knee jerk reaction from you. Even girls can have the same reaction. However, the lines begin to blur when you don't just physically react to the pain of this person but you experience a corresponding pain in your nether region as well. The guys who conducted this research say that it is so rare that only about 2 percent of the population experience this.

This got me really interested because I have had a personal experience that I would say fit into this phenomenon. This was this period that I went to visit one of my very close cousins. I spent a few days at their home and the wife was very pregnant at the time. It was not one of those celebrity type pregnancies with the glowing skin and all-round gorgeousness. She had morning sickness, back pain, and acne on her face and body. I felt so sorry for her that at the end of my first day, I was puking a lot. At first, we thought that I had come down with the flu or something. I was quarantined in my room but at the end of day two, it was clear that I was mirroring her symptoms as I suddenly had acne on my face and chest. This was an isolated incident and I never gave it much thought after that period. But reading up on this research brought that to mind. Anyway, back to the research.

The gist of it was that they handed out materials to random people to assess their empathy levels and then a short test was conducted on them. The test was pretty straight-forward. The subject was to sit down and then a finger would tap one side of their face while they watched another person being tapped on their face also except it is on the opposite side. Then they were asked where they felt the tap. The general theory is that people who have the mirror-touch synesthesia were hesitant in responding because they were unsure where they felt the tap. Now the results were not entirely conclusive in supporting the existence of empaths. However, they showed us an aspect of empathy that may explain why certain people are highly 'empathic' than others. The inability to distinguish between one's own personal experience from that of others is a disturbing concept and clearly needs to be studied further but it does highlight the traits. My major takeaway from the results of that research is that there is an element of choice in the process. There isn't a brain design flaw that makes you more or less prone to being empathetic. And I think that all three types of research in a way support this. A part of you will react to certain situations a little differently than other people would but at the end of the day, this is not something you are doing without the participation of your will. In other words, empaths are not born empaths. It is a process. A combination of your upbringing, personal values and sometimes, a touch of biology.

That said, I did promise to look at one of the not so conventional scientific explanation behind the existence of empaths. I read a lot of articles on the subject and this particular one stood out for me. According to them, [I am not even going to waste your time by sending you over there with a link to read it] empaths are people who suffer from sensory processing disorder. If you spilled your coffee as you read that, you would be forgiven. But brace yourself, there is more. You see, they believe that empaths are people who are unable to accurately sort through the experiences that they get from the world around them because they are so sensitive to everything from sights to sounds and even smells. To paraphrase, "when life gets too overstimulating...some people even report dizziness, as well as increased anxiety". I had a very hard time relating to this as I am sure you would too. But after reading their description of empathic behaviors, it made sense that this would make sense to them. According to them [paraphrasing again], "enhanced empathy is the emotional equivalent of feeling pain at the gentlest touch on your arm". I would file this under 7234 things that an empath is not.

In conclusion, according to science, being an empath does not make you an oddball. You may react to things differently but that is just a part of what makes you special.

The Difference Between Cognitive, Emotional and Compassionate Empathy

When I started this journey a few years back to try and get a clear definition of what being is and what it should mean to me, I was fortunate to meet some amazing people in the process. One of them was and remains to this day a very good friend of mine. I meant Austin back in my college years right after I had come to a conclusion about science being unable to dispute the existence of empaths, the next step was to figure out how to get a handle on the whole thing and by that, I mean understanding us better. This friend of mine said one of the most profound things about being an empath. He said being an empath is like having a neural link to everyone you meet, see, hear or know about. Of course, it was a very nerdy thing to say but it was profound nonetheless. Empaths are connected to people by their emotional experiences. If this is the case, are all empaths cut from the same cloth? I mean, what happens to the empath with all these connections? How do they react? Do they experience things the same way? These questions got us thinking, if there is nothing scientifically that can differentiate one empath from another, there has to be a way to get to understand what makes empaths in general tick. And we started exploring the behavior of empaths.

Empaths react to emotions but how they react is what makes them unique. In my research, there are several types of empathy but I am going to focus on three different types (we will look at a few others later). And from these differentiations, I believe we are able to find the answers to why we act the way that we do. I will explore and explain each type one after the other and then we would bring it back to how all of that correlates with what we know about empaths.

Cognitive Empaths

These are empaths whose empathic abilities are tied to perspective. For them, the empathic experience has more to do with the fact that they are able to see things from the view of the person that they are empathizing with. Of all the three types of empathy I have come across, I think that cognitive empathy is the most detached form of empathy (well as detached as an empath can be) and it is also the most passive form of empathy. Empaths who fall in this category would make excellent mediators or diplomats as they have a propensity to see the view from both sides of the fence.

People who don't understand cognitive empaths think that they are logical emotionless beings who stick to the facts and ignore everything else but the opposite is the case. When these guys tell you that they understand how you feel, you better believe them because they actually do. Beyond emotions, a cognitive empath makes genuine effort to really "get" where you are coming from by deliberately taking a mental work in your shoes. And when they are in those shoes, they immerse themselves in the situation so that they can feel everything that you are feeling. I think that their response to people's emotional distress is less reactive and more pragmatic. And not pragmatic in the general sense of the word. Their practical approach to a solution would stem from their clear vision of where you are coming from.

For example, when a cognitive empath is proffering a solution to say a homeless person, it is going to go beyond a can of soup. And this is because they see the problem as a whole and not just the momentary discomforts that the person is currently experience. A typical cognitive empath would put themselves in the entire journey of a homeless person. They would look at the migration pattern of the homeless person, look at the weather conditions of the areas they are most likely going to spend the night, the hassle of moving around from place to place but without the luxury of having assorted clothes to match the seasons. So, you would find them doing something like buying or even designing a flexible outfit that can adapt to different weather conditions without requiring much maintenance. Not many people would this decision but after reading up on them, it made sense that the solution would be so practical but born from a place of understanding.

Emotional Empathy

This type of empathy is pretty much self-explanatory but to ensure that we are all on the same page, I am going to get into it anyway. Emotional empathy is an instinctive form of empathy where the empath reacts to the emotions of other people. Psychological profilers refer to this type of empathy as the most primitive form of empathy. If you go over what we discussed in the section that focused on the scientific theories behind empathy, that mirror effect that was highlighted in one of the studies is very applicable here.

An emotional empath may mirror the emotion that they see or hear in other people. But their emotional reaction does not always come from a place of logical understanding. It is just a reflex. However, just because it does not appear to be a thought-out process does not mean that emotional empaths are clueless about their reactions. As a matter of, the emotional quotient of emotional empaths is unusually high. They would be having a conversation with you and based their interpretation of certain body languages and the vibes (for lack of a better word) that you give off, they can pick on what you are feeling and mirror either the same emotion or a corresponding emotion that would make you feel better. The general scope is that these guys are very emotionally intelligent.

One very common misconception people have about emotional empaths is that they are very emotional and would probably cry or lose control of their emotions at the drop of the hat. The reality is different. Their emotional intelligence affords them the ability to also sense their own emotions and then put a stopper on it before it gets out of hand. They can accurately detect emotions, reflect those emotions and sometimes even deflect those emotions before the person experiencing them even realizes what is going on. They have this innate gift of being able to make the people around feel better.

Compassionate Empathy

Now, this right here is the most active form of empathy. It combines aspects of both the cognitive empathy and the emotional empathy in that the compassionate empath is able to see things from the other person's point of view and then react based on the understanding that they now have. The emotional empath is the guy that we all know and have stereotyped as the typical empath while the compassionate empath is the one who we are all trying to become. The qualities of the compassionate empath almost put them on that celestial level because they sound almost too good to be true but that is who they are essentially.

An compassionate empath is the kind of person who would know that her best friend's heartbreak playlist is a sign that all in not well in the romance department and more than just acknowledging that this is what is going on, they would take it a step further by organizing just the right kind of event or activity that would get the said friend out of their funk and into a new groove. We all want a compassionate empath in our corner because they make life that much easier to navigate.

Now looking back on these three empaths, you would see that they each have their advantages and disadvantages (some more than the other) but they all serve a purpose. The end goal for empaths is to become the compassionate empath because they seem to have a healthy balance of action and reactions. One thing I observed across the board is that you can work towards improving aspects of yourself if you feel that you lean too much in one category. For instance, if you find that you are too pragmatic in your dealings with people, you may want to train yourself to be more emotionally intelligent. Don't get me wrong. I don't think that being practical is wrong. But sometimes, you can get a little too disconnected from the present reality because you are so focused on the bigger picture. A little emotional intelligence would go a long way in fixing this. As for the emotional empath, sometimes, the people around you are going to need more than a show of feelings to get them through situations. Getting to understand what they are really going through rather than relying on your instincts alone can help you be more 'useful' in times of crisis.

What makes an empath?

At the end of the first segment in this chapter, there was one big lesson we learned about what empaths are not… they are not created even though in some cases, they are born the way they are (very confusing, I know= but we will get to that in a bit). Granted, there are some biological markers that would play a role in how you process certain things, however, it does not ultimately define you. One of the biological factors attributed to certain empathic behaviors is the amygdalae. The science guys tell us that empaths have their amygdalae a little bit bigger than those of their average counterpart but there has also been some talk about people with larger amygdalae having deep seethed anxiety issues. According to that research, certain events (related to fear and anxiety) can trigger a growth of new cells in this area of the brain which in turn increases the size of this part of the brain leading to more anxiety. Seeing as empaths are not exactly riddled with anxiety, you can't blame biology for this one.

Some people try to trace their empathic abilities to a particular event, trauma or memory in their lives despite the fact that they are unable to remember a time when they were never the way they are now. Admitting to abilities being caused or triggered by some kind of tragedy would imply that the abilities were dormant and somehow, they were woken. Not only does this sound unrealistic, but it also sounds like something that was ripped off the plot of a low-budget sci-fi movie… cryptic, bizarre and false. If nothing else, the opposite happens. A tragic event can trigger a shut down of your empathic abilities. In subsequent chapters, we will discuss this in detail but take it from me, empathy is not born out of one's personal experience. I should point out here that there are certain experiences you would have that would cause you to empathize with anyone who goes through something similar. However, as I am sure we have learned so far, the display of empathy is not what automatically makes you an empath. There is more to it than that.

Until scientific research proves otherwise, rather than looking for one element as the spark that set off the who empathic nature in motion, think of your existence as the result of many factors coming together to create one awesome you. There is a biological component there to kick things off, a smidgen of experiences to open you up to more emotions, a little bit of social conditioning and a healthy dose of willpower.

5 other types of empaths you didn't know about

When we got into this segment about the different types of empaths, I did say we would look at other types of empaths. If you were unable to identify with the other forms of empathy, there is a great chance that you just might find your fit here. Mind you, these types of empaths are not very common but they have very unique identifiable traits and I will go over those traits briefly.

Geomantic Empath: The emotions of a geomantic empath is attuned to the environment that they are in. Their empathic abilities feed off the energies of whatever location they find themselves in. A typical geomantic empath would tell you that certain places make them feel a specific kind of emotion. They are usually drawn to places that either has a rich history or places that are considered sacred like temples, churches and so on.

Plant Empath: These guys have what we all call a green thumb and this is because plants always seem to thrive better under their care. But that has more to do with their natural intuition for the needs of the plants than their knowledge about planting itself. Plant empaths tend to thrive in jobs or businesses that revolve around the plant industry.

Animal Empath: Like the plant empaths, animal empaths are attuned to the needs of animals. They can somehow sense what animals need. The common term for them is animal whisperers. However, unlike plant empaths who connects with almost all kinds of plants, animal empaths are likely attuned to a specific animal. So, it is not out of the ordinary to find animal empaths whose empathy is towards cats, dogs or even birds.

Intuitive Empath: Also called claircognizant empaths, these guys can intuitively pick up on the emotions of other people without being told about them. They are the kind of empaths who are not easily swayed by the emotional expressions of people because they can sense the true nature of the person's emotions hidden underneath the façade that they present no matter how well constructed it is.

Physical/Medical Empath: A medical empath can almost immediately sense when a person's body is out of order for health reasons. They pick up on the energy coming off people that they meet and they can read that energy the same way a meteorologist would read the weather.

Chapter Three - The Empath Reality

After looking at empathy and the empath from both a mythical and scientific point, it is time to get real with what this is all about. And by real, I mean getting to the nitty-gritty details of the everyday life of an empath. Beyond the digital hype that has been amplified by the media's portrayal of empaths, there is the reality and it is not always pleasant. This reality is the reason you probably picked up this book in the first place. The 'gift' of seeing the world through the multi-colored lenses of emotions comes at a price. And the sooner you understand the price you are paying, the easier it would be to stop the spiral down the proverbial rabbit hole. As you read further, you may have to confront some startling truths. It may get a little uncomfortable but I promise you that it gets better in the end. Instead of looking at this as a forecast of doom, think of it as your private coming out party where you get to see yourself reflected in the pages of this book in all of your shining glory… flaws, strengths and all.

The Dark Side of Being an Empath

We know that empaths are generally emotionally intuitive on some level even if what they are attuned to might be different. However, this experience leaves them emotionally raw and sensitive most of the time. But emotional sensitivity is not the only thing that they have to deal with. Reflecting on my life as well as the information I was able to put together during my research, I made a list of a few of the things that almost all empaths would struggle with.

1. Empaths have a tendency to become depressed: For empaths, it is a constant battle to sort through the myriad of emotions that they feel. First, they have to work hard at keeping their emotions in check. As I have established, most empaths are emotionally intelligent and as a result, you won't find them losing control of their emotions but what most people do not realize is how difficult it is to do this. After putting a lid on their emotions, the next thing they have to do is determine if the emotions that they are struggling with is their own in the first place. Given their ability to absorb the emotions of other people, it is understandable that those feelings can eventually become mixed up with their own personal opinions and emotions. These frequent internal battles can lead to depression.

2. Empaths are typically emotionally exhausted: Dealing with emotions at the frequency and intensity that empaths do is very draining. This leads to an emotional fatigue

3. Empaths treat themselves as second class citizens: I am not sure if this is tied to the depression or the fact that they are always at the brink of exhaustion. But most empaths operate their personal lives on reserve because of all the other stuff that they have to deal with. Their impulsive need to help other people make it difficult for them to prioritize themselves.

4. Empaths struggle with guilt: Helping people is primal instinct for empaths. When they are confronted by any emotional puzzle, they have an almost compulsive need to put the pieces together and, in a situation where they fail to do so, they take this as a personal loss. They feel that they have failed the person or persons involved and this guilt could eat at them for a very long time. Sometimes, they task themselves with making up for this perceived failure by bending over backward to please and appease the "wronged" person.

5. Empaths are emotional sponges: Soaking up the energy of a room might sound cool until you find yourself soaking up more negative energy than a person should have to deal with. And while empaths have the ability to turn off the emotional faucet just as fast as they turn it on, their guilt-ridden nature makes them more inclined to deal with the negative stuff that people put out for longer than the average human. Coping with negative people is one thing but taking on some aspects of that negativity, that is a different ball game entirely and not a fun one at that. This brings us to the next big issue.

6. Empaths have a tendency to be in toxic relationships: Every one of the traits that we have looked at so far bring s us to this point. Because of the giving nature of the empath, they tend to attract the kind of people who would deliberately take advantage of that. And even when an empath is in a relationship where they are being taken advantage of, you would be hard-pressed to find them getting out of that situation willingly. Some of those who have successfully left those relationships end up guilt-tripping themselves back into those toxic situations.

These dark traits attributed to empaths does not essentially mean that all empaths have to be this way. In other words, you don't have to live with the darkness. However, there are certain behavioral patterns that have to be dealt with in order to deal with the darkness. Being an empath may make you prone to certain things like the depression we talked about but there are habits that you have that could drive your life to the point where everything that you do is characterized by depression. In this next segment, we are going to be looking at some of those habits.

5 Bad Habits that Empaths Must Let Go

1. Saying yes to everything: Empaths are natural people pleasers. This makes them more inclined to say yes even when that yes does not benefit them in any way. In the workplace, this can leave the empath stuck in a career rut as they find themselves spending more hours completing other people's project instead of focusing on growing their careers.

2. The need to fix everything: The phrase, "if it is not broke, don't fix it' tends to fly over the head of an empath. A bird with broken wings needs to be nursed back to health, a child with a sad history needs a

little light to let go of that dark past but a grown person with deep anger management issues need to make the choice to be better and no amount of loving or caring can get them to that place without their own consent. Empaths need to know when to leave things well alone.

3. Not speaking up for themselves: Empaths are no pushovers. At least not in the basic sense of it. However, they like to leave the floor open to other people to air their views and feelings while their own feelings are out in the back burner. This is born out of goodwill as they feel that the other person venting would help them release whatever they are feeling but it becomes a burden if you as an empath frequently have to hold back on saying how you really feel. This leads to a lot of repressed emotions which we know is a mental ticking time bomb.

4. Choosing to spend more time in their head: It is okay to step back every other day and take a few moments to be with yourself. But when it becomes a regular habit, it can be detrimental to you. It actually makes sense that you want to avoid dealing with all those emotions which come as part of the package when you have to deal with people. However, if you let go of most of the habits listed here, you would find it a lot easier to deal with people.

5. Taking things too personally: When you are sensitive and are an emotional sponge, everything that happens around you may begin to feel like it is all about you. Certain harmless comments or actions may be interpreted as a vendetta directed at you. I would say that has a lot to do with your need to piece together emotional puzzles, therefore, everything would seem connected to something which is then translated into personal meaning. But the truth is, things happen simply because they just happen.

The 5 Common Health Problems of Empaths

For the most part, due to the highly emotional nature of an empath, their health struggles are more psychological and mental than they are physical. So, a lot of things you would see in this segment have more to do with the mental illnesses than anything else. However, the lifestyle of the empath could influence the health issues they face more than their nature as empaths. Still, we cannot ignore the role that their nature plays in the process.

1. Anxiety: Most empaths battle with anxiety. The level of anxiety that they suffer varies from mild to severe and emotional empaths tend to have the most severe cases of anxiety when compared to others. Physical empaths are another group of empaths whose anxiety levels soar through the roof especially if they have to deal with crowds but it often veers into another mental health territory like panic disorders and we will get to that in a bit. Their ability to overcome or at least manage their anxiety is largely dependent on their self-awareness about who they are.

2. Depression: Given their propensity to juggle emotions at the same time, it is not surprising that they also have to deal with issues of depression from time to time. When they are not picking up on other people's emotions, they have to deal with guilt, isolation and their own personal drama. It is almost as if they can't catch a break. In addition to being self-aware, empaths need to talk with fellow empaths or therapist to help them sort through their emotions.

3. High Blood Pressure: High blood pressure is strongly linked to lifestyle and diet. However, stress and anxiety (which we know empaths are prone to) have been known to cause temporary spikes in blood pressure. The effect of anxiety on blood pressure does not last long but if it happens regularly, this blood pressure spikes can go ahead to cause damage to major organs in the body. Empaths should learn relaxation techniques that would help them bring their blood pressure down when they have an anxiety attack. Also, they need to watch out for the kind of habits they pick up to cope with anxiety. Habits like smoking can go on to complicate their health.

4. Panic Disorders: This usually happens when a person's stress and anxiety levels experienced are soaring really high. This is brought on by stressful situations and for empaths, this typically means when they are surrounded by a lot of people with all of these emotions hitting them from different directions. Panic disorders are not necessarily life-threatening but the experience is horrible. Seeking the help of a medical professional goes a long way in the treatment and management of panic disorders.

5, Agoraphobia: Everyone has some form of phobia but there are phobias that are peculiar to people with certain traits. Agoraphobia is a form of anxiety that causes a person to be afraid of being in crowded spaces or places where they get a sense that they cannot escape. Agoraphobia is best treated in its early stages. The more it is left unattended, the more overpowering it comes. It is not life-threatening in the physical sense but it can rob you of living a fulfilled life. The experience is so much worse for an empath.

As you have read, the health issues of an empath are somewhat interrelated. Again, your lifestyle does play an important role in how healthy you are. But having a very good understanding of your personality as an empath and being very self-aware as to how things really work for you would go a long way to helping you establish a good foundation for a healthy life. As you have seen, prevention is way better than treatment for most of the ailments here. The general assumption is that it is specific situations that trigger these ailments and while that is true, that is not the only trigger out there. There are people who are classified as 'toxic' especially for an empath. These people are not necessarily evil but their behavior, mannerisms and personality traits make the life of an empath more complicated than it should be. So, in keeping with the theme of prevention, let us look at a few personalities you should definitely avoid as an empath.

The Personalities that Empaths Can't be Around

Narcissists:

These personality types are so into themselves that they would fail to see the harm their neglect and selfishness is causing the empath in their lives. Their actions may not be out of malice but the sensitive empath should not have to deal with this daily. It becomes even worse when the person is an abusive narcissist.

Manipulators:

This is another breed of selfish personalities who are willing to go the extra mile to make the people around them do the things that they want to do even if those things benefit no one else but themselves. Manipulators would play on the guilt that empaths feel to get them to do their bidding. This creates a very toxic cycle for the empath.

Abusers:

Nobody should be around abusers but this is especially true for empaths. Most abusers combine the traits of a narcissist and a manipulator in addition to their personal insecurities and constant need for control. An empath is actually the one person who can connect well enough with an abuser to even see things from their perspective and in a sad way, understand where they are coming from well enough to dare, I say it, justify the abuse that they are suffering. No one should have to go through that.

Chapter Four - The Injured Empath

In the first chapter, I shared some of the biggest misconceptions that people have about empaths. One of them was the idea that empaths are broken people; that for them to be able to connect to the feelings and experiences that a lot of people have, they must have walked the same path. By now, you know that this isn't the case. An empath does not need to have a first-hand experience to truly understand what you feel. However, through their abilities, they can get front row seats to your pain and know exactly how it feels. That said, it does not mean that there are no broken empaths. Being broken is part of the human experience and as long as you are human, you are bound to have a phase where you are broken. The loss of something of value whether an object, a person or even ideas that we have can cause a pain so intense that you feel crushed by the weight of it. This is the point where a person gets broken.

There is absolutely nothing wrong in being broken. The problem comes when you let that experience characterize everything that you do going forward. You have to understand that it is a human nature to fall, but it is also our nature to rise. Now rising does not necessarily mean that everything would right back to status quo. When you fall down and get injured, it hurts. Physiologically, a few cells die in the area where the injury occurred. But as the body begins the healing process, a few new cells are born. As the healing progresses, the pain begins to recede until all that is left to remind you of the injury is the scar. In the same manner, when life kicks us down, we get hurt and broken. But if you let it, the brokenness heals as begin to rise. However, we are left with the scars of those experiences. If the memories from those experiences are not brought into focus and the emotions that were stirred at that point in time not addressed, the emotional scars that will develop can affect the quality of life as well as the opportunities that you have later on.

An injured person is one carries the emotional scars from their past wherever they go. For an injured empath, the experience is even worse they are relieving these emotions at intensity levels that are so high that the past would seem like it only just happened yesterday. Each moment brings them a visit from the past and cages them in the present so that they are oblivious to the joys that are going on and unable to move forward to the future that they deserve. Injured empaths are curiously like the Mimosa Pudica also known as the touch me not plant. The second you touch them; their leaves close up. Incidentally, another nickname for the touch me not plant is 'the sensitive plant'. Their reaction to touch is the same way that an injured empath would react to life. Their emotional scars are so deep and the effect is so intense that every time life singles them out for a new experience whether good or bad, they quickly recoil to the 'safe' haven that they have created for themselves. The sad part is that this so-called safe haven is anything but safe. It is like a room with a living breathing nuclear reactor in it that draws its energy from the darkness surrounding it.

Another sad fact is that like the average person, most empaths won't even realize what is happening to themselves until either they are consumed by their past (an emotional nuclear explosion) or something disrupts the cycle of behavior that led down that destructive path, to begin with. It doesn't help that the coping mechanisms for most empaths are self-destructive behaviors, to begin with. For starters, there is that reclusive behavior. There is nothing wrong in being a recluse, but you take things to the extreme when paranoia sets in and you begin to hide even from your own shadow. The only way forward is to allow our minds to heal and recover from the emotional injuries sustained. When a physical wound is being treated, the very first thing any doctor would do is to make an attempt to treat the life-threatening symptoms of the wound. For emotional injuries, I would say the equivalent of that is coming out of your shell. Even if you are going to stay inside of your house cooped up, the least you can do is to pick up the phone and call somebody and then just talk. It does not have to be about what you are going through. The fact that you are having a conversation alone is going to be like coming up for a breath of fresh air after in an oxygen-deprived space.

The next step is to go the source of the wound which in the case of an empath is not always the incident that you think triggered the pain in the first place. It is usually something called compassion fatigue. And that is what the rest of this chapter is going to be about.

What is Compassion Fatigue?

In very lay terms, compassion fatigue happens when a person becomes emotionally desensitized to the needs, pains and sufferings of other people. Compassion fatigue is also known as secondary traumatic stress and has been associated with people who have been constantly exposed stories and experiences of tragedies for so long that it would appear as though their nerve endings just snapped and stopped functioning. Now, you may be inclined to think that this means the person experiencing the compassion fatigue (in this case an empath) would move from their end of the scale and tip towards the section where you have the psychopaths. This is not so. People who suffer from compassion fatigue don't suddenly become dead to their emotions. In fact, they become even more acutely aware of it. what happens is that they internalize these emotions that they feel and are unable or unmotivated to act on it.

Let me give you a brief rundown of my theory on the subject. When you are confronted with a situation where a person that you know on some level is going through a very tragic experience, you are instinctively inclined to want to help. You find a way to provide a solution for that person. Even if you cannot completely avert the tragedy, you want to do all that you can to improve the situation. When you achieve this, there is a reward section of your brain that is triggered. You feel very good about this good deed that you are done. In that moment, the sun shines a little brighter, the world appears to have a little more color and life, in general, is very fantastic. This perhaps explains people have been trying to convince us that doing good does some with its own special kind of reward. This is all good and well. After living through this wonderful experience which essentially is a psychological feedback from your good deed, you are inclined to repeat this process again. It doesn't matter if the circumstances are the same or different, you want to help this new person. For empaths, this experience can be very addictive. They want to keep doing these good deeds and continue reliving the psychological aftermath. It is like a high except that there is no drug that can quite match the effect. But when happens when the good deed that you carried out is unable to make a difference?

This is where the story takes a slightly darker turn. Let us take this same scenario we mentioned earlier but with a not so positive outcome. You are confronted with a situation where someone you know on some level is going through some kind of tragic experience. As a good friend, colleague or whatever your relationship is with that person, you step in to help because that is just what you do. Now you offer this help in the hope that the tragedy can be averted or in the very least, the circumstance can be improved but instead, nothing happens. Or even worse, things become even more tragic than you met them. You are now forced to watch this person live through the pain and trauma from their experience until it either ends their life or ends your relationship with them. As an empath, you would get some feedback from their pain and this registers on your psyche. It doesn't stop you from trying to help people but there is a part of you that struggles with the following;

1. Your failure to help this person

2. Your second-hand experience of their pain
3. Your anxiety losing another friend or relationship in the same way

Things get a little more complicated for empaths who work in specific professions where they are constantly faced with tragedy. For empaths who have to deal with this occasionally with their circle of friends, the progression of compassion fatigue is slower. But for people whose occupations are in the health sector like nurses, care-givers, psychology and so on, there is a high risk of developing compassion fatigue within a shorter timeframe. People who work as lawyers as also susceptible to it. Empaths in these fields sometimes end up being unable to differentiate their work life from their personal lives to you would find the emotional burn out affection their ability to connect emotionally with other people too.

Having all of this in mind, you cautiously approach other relationships. Now, we all know that at some point, life happens. This other relationship may not have the same tragic elements as the previous but even the slightest hint at tragedy might get your instincts kicking in on overdrive. Obviously, you rush in to help. This time around, you are just as anxious about the results of your efforts as you are about the person's wellbeing that even if your effort is rewarded by an aversion of tragedy, your only psychological reward would be relief that all works out. The rush is not the same this success would seem to highlight your failure. And this drives you into a cycle where you keep trying to make up for the proverbial one that got away. If your effort to help fails like the first time around, you are flung deeper into that cycle and anxiety takes deeper roots in your psyche. The more fixes and saves you do, the more you want to do, but this is no longer inspired by the high which we talked about initially. It is now about balancing the scales. The stress and anxiety that comes with each case that you face pushes you closer to the line where it is no longer about helping people but simply getting through the day. At this point, you are having secondary traumatic stress.

Signs of an Injured Empath

The point where an empath experiences compassion fatigue is where the emotional injury we discussed earlier is rooted. As I said, it is not isolated to an event or a singular experience so you cannot take a mental trip to this specific spot, snap your fingers and find closure. It is a little more complicated than that. Thankfully, you can determine if you have arrived at this point even though you don't know what led you here. If you recall, I painted a picture of a safe haven likened to a room housing an active nuclear reactor and how toxic that environment can be for you. In this section, we are going to highlight all these factors that make being in the state where you are dangerous and then we will talk about how to cross those hurdles.

1. A Keen Sense of Hopelessness that Results in Detachment

If you find yourself unable to summon a genuine feeling of optimism for the things that you do, you may have subscribed to that feeling of hopelessness. When you have a situation that requires your help and you do it not because you are certain or in the very least hoping that it would make a difference, but because you are obligated to, you might be having compassion fatigue. In this case, the need to play out your role takes priority over the needs of the person. Everything about caring for this person becomes a routine activity for you. The biggest clue in this regard would be the fact that you are unable to look past today because you feel that there is a very strong possibility that there won't be a tomorrow.

2. Apathy Toward the People You Care for

This is a form of detachment but not necessarily an absence of care because as an empath on some level, you always care. But the experiences you have had has groomed you to the point that you have become indifferent to the entire experience. You are more matter-of-factly in the way you care and help. Since your indifference does not come from a place of malice or ill will, you will always show up. However, your indifference has been constructed as a wall to protect you from the tragedy you are already expecting so that 'when' it happens, you are not so visibly affected by it. If you find yourself thinking this way, know that you are probably experiencing compassion fatigue

3. Elevated Stress Levels

In the face of tragedy, we experience a lot of things emotionally. These emotions cause stress. Now there is the normal stress level of the average person and then you have abnormal stress levels. Compassion fatigue triggers a high level of stress even in situations that have very little similarities to the events that you can call the ground zero of your emotional trauma. In addition to all the other symptoms mentioned here, if you discover that you are reacting adversely to stress such as breathlessness, inability to focus, severe anxiety and panic attacks, you are having compassion fatigue

4. Nightmares and disruption in sleep routines

Nightmares and a change in sleep routine is typically a sign of an internal struggle with some kind of unresolved emotional trauma. When dealing with the pain of other people trigger nightmares and sleeplessness, it is possible that you are having an emotional burnout. Your mind is unable to cope with the situation and even worse, it is unable to cope with the fact that you cannot cope with the situation… a classic nightmare for empaths.

5. Struggling with feelings of Self-Contempt

Empaths already have a thing for guilt-tripping themselves. When they hit the compassion fatigue point, this guilt grows into self-contempt as they feel a sense of disappointment in their inadequacies. This is because empaths measure their sense of self-worth with their ability to provide help and 'fix' things. Failure to do this causes self-doubt which evolves into guilt and grows into contempt.

If you look at all of the symptoms listed, you would see the progression of the internal struggle brought on by compassion fatigue. An outward experience becomes an inward struggle that becomes all about them which can be pretty selfish and a strong contradiction to their normally selfless nature. The inward struggle is what keeps them in that 'room' we talked about earlier. They find it difficult to come of this mental space that they have created because they have adorned themselves with the persona of a victim. Somehow, this thing that totally was about them has now made them the victim. In the next chapter, we discuss this in detail.

Beware: The Victim Complex

Self-pity is a normal experience for everyone. We have moments when we fall into that woe-is-me hole but as long as you don't hold on to that hat for longer than necessary, you are going to be fine. Victim complex, on the other hand, is choosing to lay on a bed of misery, covering up yourself with your failures or the list of everything that has gone wrong and just lying there in it. For an empath, having a case of compassion fatigue can create a segue into a full-blown victim complex experience. The general experience of the victim complex would see the person experiencing it deferring all responsibility to everyone and everything but themselves. But in the case of the empath, they take the whole blame for everything and then somehow make the entire experience about them. I know that this seems a little confusing but let me explain it anyway.

An empaths victim complex is not about making themselves the star of the show by abdicating any blame or responsibility that was assigned to them. They don't wear the sad-is-me crown to make other people feel sorry for them. If anything, they would hate to be that person because there is a very strong possibility that they deal with such people on a regular basis. The victim complex for empaths come in when they internalize their failures, store up the pain that they have absorbed on the outside and then sort of idolize it on the inside. Most injured empaths have a victim complex. They do not have the resilience needed to cope with their personal failures. Now let me digress a little bit here. A personal failure for an empath goes beyond their inability to successfully complete a project. That kind of failure is one that they can deal with. But when they are unable to fix their people projects, that kind of failure seeps deep into their minds and they take it personally. They can get so fixated on it that they work twice as hard to 'redeem' themselves with other people projects.

Besides the increased risk of failure associated with taking on more people project, there is the problem of not dealing with the initial failure. As a result, any people project that is taken on would only echo the failure and the longer they deal with this, the more intense the situation would get. The intensity of the emotions experienced would lead to an emotional burn out that we have now identified as compassion fatigue which leads us to where we are now. A victim complex sounds like something harmless but here is the part I am pretty sure that you did not know. The victim complex is the element that keeps the wheels spinning in this self-destructive cycle. It is the bars that would keep you locked in that 'safe' room that stops you from living your life. I read of an ancient religious group where believers or practitioners were physically chastised whenever they err. These chastisements were so terrible that they would be in physical pain for months on end. The scars that they bore on their bodies told tales of horror and trauma so horrendous that you would think that they served in slaves camps or some kind of torture chamber. The reality was that all of these injuries were self-inflicted.

The need to make yourself pay for perceived failures by locking up yourself in this 'safe' haven is the emotional equivalent of the self-inflicted injuries on those believers. Take your freedom today by learning to prioritize your self-care just as much as you value the care of other people. Most importantly, you need to stop looking at people as projects that you need to fix. I have mentioned this before and later in the book, we would discuss this in-depth. But if you do anything today, let it be that you acknowledge your importance and treat yourself accordingly. That said, I would like us to look at another self-destructive behavior that could ruin the life of an empath

The Truth About Empaths and Addiction

The emotional turmoil, as well as the intrinsic nature of the empath, make them a perfect candidate for addiction. Their need to get out of their own heads every other day means they are open to trying out coping mechanisms that would offer them this. The fact that this emotional turmoil is an ongoing struggle means that they are more likely to keep going back to continue using this coping mechanism especially if it successfully provides the temporary fix that they need. When you try something for so long, it becomes a routine. Over time, a routine becomes a habit and with habits, especially bad habits, you get addicted. A coping mechanism could be anything from drug use to comfort eating to watching porn. And the thing with these things I have mentioned is that you never really see it as a problem until it is too late.

In my experience, food was my vice. It started out innocently enough. I would come back home from work, tired and exhausted. However, no matter how exhausted I was, sleep was something that eluded me. So, I would get out of bed, fix myself something sweet in the kitchen and then plop myself down on the couch and binge-watch those terrible television shows. In those moments, I was completely calm, very relaxed and certainly not thinking about the horrible day I had at work. After some time, I decided to upgrade my couch meal to something with a more 'luxurious' feel. I would stop by at the pastry shop on my way home and pick up an array of sweet treats and then repeat my routine in front of the TV. A few months later, the couch didn't feel comfortable enough so I got a larger screen and then took the show into my bedroom. For the better part of a year, I spent my nights eating junk food in bed while watching junk TV. As you can imagine, it started showing on my waistline. My old clothes stopped fitting me and then I started feeling more self-conscious about how I looked.

I had friends who were too polite to point out the physical changes but I could see the way they looked at me. Then I had 'friends' who had no problems telling me exactly how they felt. Their words made me feel even more horrible about myself and when I felt really bad, it meant I spent a lot more at the pastry shop. My lowest point which also turned out to be my turning point was this particular day when I was eating this really delicious donut on my way home (it had gotten to the point that I couldn't wait to get home anymore). The donut slipped from my hand and fell on the floor. It was probably around 7 pm and there weren't that many people on the street. I know because I glanced around and then I did the unthinkable. I bent down and pick my fallen donut off the sidewalk. I blew on it and ate it with I was still bent there with one knee on the floor. Just then, I caught my reflection in one of the storefronts and I did not like the person who was starring back at me. To make a long story short, I had a good cry when I got home and that was the beginning of my journey to this point where I am writing my story in a book. Today, I still have an addiction but I have made a conscious effort to ensure that my addiction is healthy. I have a habit for different moods. When I am angry, I paint. When I feel a little blue, I get on the treadmill or put on my boxing gloves and work up a good sweat. When I am anxious, I write.

You are going to have to find out what works for you but it starts with you admitting to yourself that this seemingly harmless habit you have engaged may not be entirely healthy for you. People think that drug is the only harmful addiction, I have read about empaths who are addicted to the misery they are facing that they would willingly self-sabotage any shot that they have at happiness. It is sad to witness but this is the reality. When you are experiencing those floods of emotions, what are the things that you do to cope? Do those things add value to you as they make you feel better or do they take away something valuable from you in exchange for making you feel better? Addiction for empaths is a serious problem and it needs to be taken seriously or else you would end up complicating things for yourself. Today, the goal is to get you out of that sense of false security that you have created for yourself. This book is a guide on how you can survive in the world as an empath. For that to happen, you need to step out of your enclave and into the real world because not only will you survive it, you will thrive in it.

Chapter Five - The Dangers of Being an Empath

In the previous chapter, we explored some of the dangers of being an empath. In this chapter we are going to delve into the dark side of things. Leading up to this point, empaths have been regarded as beings in possession of supernatural power. That is cool and I honestly wished it was that way 100% of the time but there's a price that empaths and it goes beyond the emotional struggles that we have. Because of the intricate nature of the empath, they tend to attract a certain kind of people to themselves. We have talked about the need for the empath to fix people. Whenever they encounter people with emotional struggles and some psychological pain, the first instinct is to want to help but we forget that not all the people that come to us want to be helped. Some people are programmed or to be more specific, they are emotionally programmed to take advantage of the help that we wish to offer and this is where the problem begins.

The empire's desire to help attract a specific kind of people and more often than not, these people fall into the category of those with a psychological need to take advantage of others. Sometimes these relationships start out with good intentions. But in time, their predatory nature quickly takes over and they end up destroying the empath from within. This is the danger that all empaths face. In the previous chapter, I talked about certain kinds of people that empaths should avoid and one of those people is the narcissist. The narcissist is a special breed of individuals and their qualities go beyond their love for themselves. They are recognized for their skills at masterfully manipulating people to do their bidding and the nature of the empath make them more prone to the manipulations of a narcissist.

Identifying a narcissist

From old literature, we are led to believe that a narcissist is someone who is vain; a person who is obsessed with their physical looks and how they present themselves to the world. In psychology, it's a lot deeper than that as narcissist take on a different form. One of their unappealing qualities is the fact that they have a great sense of self-importance but for someone who is not very observant, this attribute is not something that you would pick on right away. Their victim mentality provides a great mask for their true personality but more importantly, they have a way of blending in perfectly with the rest of the society which makes it somewhat difficult to identify them. Some narcissists are simply harmless in their relationships. Narcissists who fall in this category are people who are self-aware and have worked on the negative side of themselves. But then you have the narcissists on the other spectrum who are terrible as companions because their sense of self-importance is so grand that they are willing to compromise the feelings and emotions of other people just to satisfy their own needs. Narcissists are selfish, self-important and self-righteous but ironically, they are the list self-aware people.

Based on the description I have given, I am sure you can understand why narcissists are people that can be very difficult to deal with even for anyone who is not an empath. However, if you're able to understand them, you get a better sense of how to relate with them especially if you are an empath. According to psychology, there are different types of narcissists. You have the grandiose narcissist. These guys are basically people who have a huge ego. To deal with them, you need to offer up a lot of attention in the form of praise. This feeds their ego and makes them much more manageable in relationships. Then you have the vulnerable narcissists. You can identify them by the victim mentality that they seem to wear like a badge. Everything that happens in life seems to revolve around them. It could be raining somewhere in China and causing floods in certain villages but the vulnerable narcissist living a few continents away would find a way to make it about them. They have a very high tendency to complain about anything and everything. To manage a relationship with them, they need to be given attention in the form of emotional support. And then finally, you have the malignant narcissists. These guys are the ones you need to watch out for. The other two types of narcissist mentioned earlier can be emotionally exhausting to deal with but as far as damages go, as long as you can give them what they want in terms of their emotional needs, they are fine. Malignant narcissists, on the other hand, display a lack of empathy on the level that is so high that psychologists compare them with psychopaths.

To identify the malignant narcissist in your life you would need to be very attentive. As I said earlier, a narcissist has a way of blending in with everyone. So, there aren't really factors that make them stand out from the crowd. In fact, psychologists believe that narcissist are usually happier than most people who have been diagnosed with some form of psychological disorder. To keep things in perspective, I compiled a list that will help you identify a narcissist specifically, the malignant narcissist. This list is based on certain traits. Be guided though, you need a clinical psychologist to accurately diagnose a malignant narcissist but until that happens, here are few red flags that should make you wary of any person who displays more than one of these traits.

1. They have a strong sense of self-importance
2. They are very obsessed with their idea of what they consider as ideal (the ideal wife, the ideal friend, the ideal love, the ideal relationship)
3. They have a very strong sense of entitlement
4. They have an unrealistic expectation about things in general
5. They have a tendency to use other people to get what they want
6. They are very manipulative
7. They lack empathy and display an unwillingness to recognize the needs and emotions of other people

There is a general saying that opposites attract. Perhaps this is the foundation of the relationship between the narcissists and an empath, because, on a surface level, it is hard to determine why someone as sensitive and generous as an empath will fall for someone as cold and calculating as a narcissist but when you explore the dynamics of the relationship it does make sense why these 2 opposites would be attracted to each other. However, this relationship can only be described as a recipe for disaster. To better understand why this continues to happen, I felt it will be important to look at why these 2 people would choose each other and to determine that, we need to look at what each personality would stand to gain from this relationship.

Why Narcissists Are Drawn to Empaths

If you look at the traits of a narcissist, you would see that for them every relationship that they get into is a one-sided business transaction designed to favor just one party. I leave you with just one guess as to who that party is. A typical malignant narcissist is very calculating and they never enter into anything without a plan on how they can take. From the onset, they can instinctively recognize people who would give them a hard time achieving their goals. They hate people that they cannot manipulate and in the workplace, or environments where they are required to team up with other people, you would find the narcissist at loggerheads with these types of people. To look at what a narcissist would be drawn to, let us take a look at how relationships work with a narcissist.

When a narcissist likes someone, they would turn on their charm on them and for a brief moment, that person would feel like they are the most special people in the world. In this timeframe, the narcissist would push back gently to get a feel of their resistance level. The weaker it is, the more they push. In this stage, they would continue to maintain their charming façade. And then when they get to a point where they are absolutely certain that this person is enthralled with them, their sadistic nature and their real intentions would start to manifest. The charming exterior that they presented would either disappear completely or be used as a form of sick reward for behavior that they consider good. This relationship pattern would play out until either the narcissist gets tired or the empaths wake up from the spell that was cast over them. In some cases, it usually ends in tragedy. That said, let us look at those characteristics that act as a magnet for narcissists.

A narcissist is drawn to someone who;

- Is very giving emotionally and physically
- Has a tendency to put the needs of other people before their own
- Doesn't stand up to people they care about
- Is not anti-social but not very social either because of their shyness
- Has a very strong sense of loyalty
- Is emotionally sensitive and somewhat fragile
- Is easily moved to act on the emotional needs of others

If you noticed, these are all common traits of empaths.

Why Empaths are Drawn to Narcissists

Why do good girls like bad boys and why do the good guys fall for really bad girls? This is the question that comes to mind when I think of empaths going out with narcissists. But after being in a relationship like this, I understand why I went out with this person. Empaths are people fixers and we are naturally drawn to people that we think new can fix. The narcissist may turn on their charm to the max but on some level, I believe that an empath can always sense the damage underneath. And it is this damage that reels us in. We feed ourselves that we are going to be that special person who fixes them and makes them as right as rain. Every single gesture that is good and right towards us goes on to cement or affirm this illusion we have created and every struggle is interpreted one of the things that we have to tolerate until we hit our goals. If we dwell on this illusion long enough, the lines between reality and fiction become blurred and that illusion becomes a living breathing reality.

The primary attraction in all this for an empath has got to be the damage persona that we sense. And then the next thing would be our need to punish ourselves when we fail at our people projects. Except in this situation, the person meting out the punishment is the narcissistic figure in our lives. I think the last piece in this puzzle would be the fact that empaths feed off emotions and the ego of a narcissist feeds off people who feed off their emotion. This appears to be a symbiotic relationship in the most unhealthy way as one party is being fed with nourishments while the other party is getting toxins.

As an empath reading this, I am sure that you would have recognized a similar pattern of behavior that was exhibited in your previous or current relationship. For those whose previous relationship showed this pattern, be thankful that you dodged a bullet. If you need to talk to a psychologist to help you heal from the damage of that relationship (there will be damages) don't hesitate to speak to someone. Get closure, find yourself again and let it go. If this is your current relationship, it might be time for you to call it quits. This is not a healthy situation for you. If you have not yet been cut off from your friends and family that you trust (this is a classic narcissist move), you need to reach out to someone and ask for an intervention. In the very least, take a temporary break from this person. Don't expect this to happen without some negative reaction from the narcissist because his or her ego would be bruised and they would want to redeem it.

Signs an Empath is with an Emotional Vampire

If you're an outside the observing the relationship dynamics between an empath and a narcissist, it is not difficult to see where the hurt is coming from and where it is going. Narcissist are emotionally draining and yet the empath remains in that relationship anyway. Being an observer of my own past relationships, I can pinpoint the exact moment where I figured things were going terribly wrong. No matter how well a narcissist presents themselves, there are signs even from the beginning. You just have to be open-minded and let go of any illusions you may have. This is the hardest part but we will talk about this in the next segment. For now, let us look at those signs that can tell you immediately that the relationship you are in is destroying you from the inside.

1. You are fighting a solo battle

For starters, you want the growth of the person more than they do. There is a general saying there you can take the horse to the water but you cannot force it to drink. Individual growth is something that we have to desire for ourselves. Now, I get that as an empath, we get to see sides of a person that not many people see because we look inwards as opposed outwards. The problem is that the person we see on the inside is the person who they have a potential to become however we look at that as a reality and we commit ourselves to that illusion. If they can't see what you see, there is nothing that can be done to change things. Recognize this.

2. Everything in your relationship seems to be about them

A relationship is a two-way street. As long as they are 2 people involved, it is important that the needs, opinions, and feelings of the parties involved are recognized an attended too equally. Anything less would mean that one party is benefiting and the other party is suffering. Empaths have a tendency to be addicted to the suffering that is usually self-inflicted. This is difficult enough not to mention unhealthy to deal with on your own but if you are in a relationship and this is what you're going through, chances are you have an emotional vampire in your life who is leeching you for everything that you have. It may be time to check out of that relationship.

3. They have a general sense of entitlement

Just because you are in a relationship with someone doesn't mean that you owe them anything. People get together for mutually beneficial reasons however, there shouldn't be any sense of entitlement as to the fulfillment of those reasons. You are your own person. What you do with your time and how you do it is exactly your business. If anyone tries to force their needs on you, that is a red flag.

4. The arrogance of the person you are dealing with borders on a power play

Some people are generally arrogant we all have our pride and egos. But when a person becomes condescending in their behavior toward you, it becomes unhealthy. You deserve to be respected as a person and a relationship where there is no respect except when you are dealing with the opinions and thoughts of the other person changes from a loving union to a slave and master type situation.

5. Your social life is being controlled by the other person

As empaths, we have our periods of isolation. However, we are not introverts by choice. We always have that circle of friends or family or people that we connect with in general. The narcissist in our lives would work hard in ensuring that we are disconnected from those people that matter to us. For them, having an empath isolated from their social network would make them more malleable to their manipulations. They also feel like there are going to be fewer interruptions this way.

How to Stop Being a Target for Emotional and Energy Vampires

From my experience, the hardest word for an empath to say which coincidentally also happens to be the magic word that can go a long way to making life significantly better for them is the word, no. Apart from the ability to say no to people. I believe that by recognizing these signs which I listed above you are putting yourself on the right track to preventing yourself from getting into toxic relationships. Now that you can spot an abusive relationship, here are a few more things you can do to protect yourself;

1. Educate yourself on the concepts of an ideal relationship

Empires tend to get into their head when it comes to relationship. Like the narcissist, they project their own perception of a relationship. Unfortunately, it is often based on their personal experiences with people. This can be wrong because most times, their relationship with people tend to have this parasitic component where one person feeds off the other person. Healthy relationships don't work that way. Today, I urge you to read up on relationship materials; go on the Internet, read books and pay attention to the healthy couples in your life. Let the things that you discover help guide you to what a healthy and normal relationship is meant to look like.

2. Don't ignore your instincts

One of the wonderful gifts that we have as empaths is the ability to accurately read people, however, when our emotions are involved, we overlook the information our instincts are trying to pass them across to us. We ignore our guts and focus instead on the illusions we have built around the relationship and when this happens, even when we see physical red flags pointing us towards the toxicity of the relationship we still choose to remain. One of the many important things you are going to learn by the time you are done reading this book is that your instinct as an empath is powerful and it is also one of the guiding forces in your life. From this point on, you have to learn to pay attention to what the inner voice is saying.

3. Stop treating people as projects that need to be fixed

When we go into a relationship, we look at a person as a task to score us some mental points if we succeed in fixing them. When a person becomes a project, we fail to see the human element and oftentimes, that human element is the ability to go dark emotionally. Having that kind of mentality often gets us in trouble because when you cease to see a person as an actual person, you would be blinded to their potential to hurt you. You get caught up in the image you have created in your head. Your weakness is your deadly attraction to people who are damaged and emotionally unstable. Recognize this and make efforts to correct it as soon as possible.

4. Get to know a person before you decide to date them

A lot of mistakes can be avoided if you take the time to know the person that you are committing yourself to. They may present a false exterior initially, but with the time you have deliberately created to get to know each other, you can successfully peel off those layers and get to see them for who they really are. This is a Golden rule for every kind of relationship but it is especially important for empaths.

5. Teach yourself to desire the best

Most empaths feel that it is conceited to want or desire good things and this is understandable as it goes against their nature which puts everyone before themselves. But if you want to avoid toxic relationships it is important that not only are you able to recognize good things and good people, you should also capable of wanting those good things for yourself. You deserve happiness. Always remind yourself that no matter how much you give of yourself, you cannot make someone that is by nature bad become good. It is like drinking poison in the hope that by the time the poison gets to your stomach, it will turn into a refreshing drink. It does not make sense.

Chapter Six - Healing the Empath Heart

I am not the kind of person who likes to indulge in self-pity but I think in this place where we are right now, it would only be fair to recognize the emotional struggle that we all go through as empaths. After decompressing everything I did in the last chapter, it just feels like this is the right time to simply put a pause on everything and inhale... breath in the moment. Life really is beautiful. And we can only enjoy it if we can get out of our heads for a moment. Because I am an empath, I understand living outside our heads is not really a luxury we can afford especially since we have to deal with people and their emotions every other day. But that is fine. We need these emotions in other to feed the gift that we have on the inside, however, as we go through these emotions it is important to have a balance where we not only let go of the painful and hurtful things that we feel, we find a way to heal our hearts.

In the first chapter of this book, I talked about some of the misconceptions that people have about empaths. One of those misconceptions is the idea that empaths are broken people. Sometimes the pain that we carry is not our pain. Remember the mirror effect? These are feelings that we absorb from other people and if we don't deal with those feelings, we could end up with a crisis on our hands. What is the point of all of this? Healing in this sense does not necessarily mean that we are broken. Healing for us is a way to sort through the emotions; a way to relax and calm are in ourselves. Healing for an empath is more than just a biological activity brought on by pain. It is a pathway to our balanced emotional well-being.

5 Healing Activities for Empaths to Relax

There are different kinds of empaths (we have looked at more than a handful of them already) and the key to their healing usually lies in their intrinsic nature. For the compassionate empath, their road to healing could probably be found in activities that reward their need to help people. So, something as simple as serving soup in a homeless shelter would be relaxing. For physical empaths, activities that involve connecting with people especially when the focus of the connection is healing would be helpful. Such activities could be either a nice body massage or a Reiki healing session. For animal empaths, just spending a day indulging in a fun activity with their favorite pets can do a lot of wonders for their mental health. These things I have mentioned are unique to the nature of the empath

However, there are simple general activities that empaths can carry out that will bring them to that place where they can start to experience healing internally. If you take anything away from this chapter, let it be the fact that the healing of an empath is not initiated by a drug or the use of a substance no matter how mild. You don't need to start doing something that could become addictive. However, I created a list of 5 general activities that can help you get to a place of calm. Use this as a guide. The goal is that at the end of the segment, you would be able to relate with more than one or two activities on that list. Remember your emotional well-being is very important. If you are going to ever enjoy your gifts as an empath, you need to learn to relax.

1. Start journaling

Journaling is a therapeutic activity that you may not realize you need. It is an excellent way to get you out of your head. If you are observant, you may have noticed that I have used this phrase "get out of your head", a lot. What I mean is getting out of that mental space where you are constantly processing emotions. I know that as an empath you need to deal with different kinds of emotions at the same time. If you keep that process inside your head especially over a long period of time, chances are you're going to end up stressed out. Not many empaths have friends that they can talk to or people who will even understand what they're going through. A Journal enables you to write out your thoughts and sort through your feelings without having to deal with the backlash of processing those various emotions. it is a relaxing experience as it gives you focus and when you have focus, you are more in control of what you feel and how it affects you.

2. Release your inner artist

This part can be a little bit difficult to understand. But this is what I mean. When you are going through one of those emotional experiences, you can take that pain and turn it into art by engaging in activities that require you to be creative. This could be an activity like writing a poem, painting or something like woodwork. Now realize this, it is not about what you create. It is about the process. From experience, this process creates what I call transference of energy. That negative emotion you are feeling is converted into a creative process that has the potential to become an art. You don't have to aspire to do something grand (that would only aggravate the stress), it could be something as simple as splashing colors on a board or playing around with words. These are very cool ways to help you again, get out of your head

3. Champion a cause you care about

You know you want to make a difference and alleviate the sufferings of people. Taking a moment to give towards a cause that is important to you can have a relaxing effect on you. If you prefer to be hands-on, you can volunteer for a few minutes or hours (depending on your schedule). The helps you take care of your "people project" instinct while giving you some appropriate distance.

4. Change your routine

Empaths are creatures of habits. They feel safe in those routines even though those routines may not be good for their mental and physical health in the long run (remember my couch and pastry experience?). Breaking from routine might sound scary but when you take the step, the result can be elating. A word of caution though. Ensure that the new routine you are signing up for is beneficial to your mental health.

5. Meditation

This list would not be complete if there wasn't a mention of meditation. If you learn how to do it right, you can induce a state of complete calm no matter how stressed out you feel. Include words of affirmation as part of your meditation routine to make the meditation experience even more relaxing. I found my peace in Reiki, an energy healing journey that I take daily.

Steps to Heal Your Emotional Triggers

Emotional triggers are events, memories, places or even words that the second you see them, it invokes a specific kind of emotional reaction. When something happens to you, our brains create neural pathways (this is why having new experiences on a regular are good for you) and when those experiences are negative, the emotion that you experienced in that moment is registered and every time something similar happens, you are immediately transported to that moment. This is why you could perceive something like say a fragrance and you are transported to a time in your childhood when someone significant in your life did something while wearing that fragrance. The emotions triggered could be good or bad, this is determined by the experience that you had.

Obviously, you would be comfortable reliving good emotions unless it gets to a point where those memories are stopping you from moving forward with your life. Negative emotions affect us in many ways and those are almost never good. Personally, I think the only good thing that comes from negative experiences are the lessons that they provide. Whatever emotions are being triggered, the fact is that you are being held back from moving on and living your best life now. The best way forward is to do the following;

Empath Survival Guide

1. Stay in the moment

Stop taking a trip down memory lane. If an event occurs that makes you think of the past, don't hold on to it. Focus on what is happening. Don't let the emotions that they bring on hold you down and more importantly, don't look at your present as your opportunity to take revenge on your past. Address the situation as it happens.

2. Don't try to control the situation

Control is an illusion and if you buy into this illusion, you increase the stress and anxiety that comes with reliving emotional triggers. Accept that you cannot control what is happening to you, you cannot control anyone involved in the situation that is messing you up, however, your experience does not have to be determined by this thing that you are going through. It sounds like a contraction but here is what I mean. You have a choice in how you feel because that is what you have control over. The happiness or sadness you feel and how long you feel those things is determined by you. So, leave the situation but control your emotion.

3. Don't run from it

There is a saying that the splash of water you run away from today could become the pool that drowns you tomorrow. It might be painful to confront our feelings. But it is in that confrontation that you will encounter the truth and you already know what they say about the truth and freedom. And this brings us to the next point.

4. Know your truth

Once upon a time, people thought that the world was flat. This stopped them from going on what would have been an amazing adventure and remained where they are because they were caged by this 'reality'. But when some brave scientists were able to disprove this theory, mankind was set free to explore the ends of the earth. Emotional triggers might be based on myths that you have fed yourself and so every time you are confronted by a situation that triggers those emotions, you are trapped in what you feel. Break the cycle by disproving those myths. The outcome may not be something that you like but whatever it is, you get to own your truth.

5. Embrace all of your peculiarities

Life is a fiery bouncy ball of unexpected twists and turns and it could hit us at any time. The people in our lives would come and go. You can't cling on to a memory or a person because you are afraid of what would happen to you after you let them go. This fear is mostly because you haven't come to a place of acceptance. You are unusual, you are unique and the experiences you have are crazy but that is what makes you exceptional. In embracing yourself, lean towards loving yourself more. When you love yourself, every other thing that happens to you is just secondary.

Powerful Techniques for Healing and Self-Protection

The default setting of any person when they feel threatened is to go to a place where they feel safe. You may not always have the luxury of running to your safe space. So, what do you do then? Stop. Take time out and chill. These powerful techniques I have learned have become a coping mechanism for me and I cannot remember a point in my life when I have been happier.

Affirmations

We are made up of the words that we speak to ourselves. If you do not speak to yourself, the words that other people speak to you would become the foundation on which your life is built. And we know that the world can be a cruel place. Some of the negative things that people say to you do not come from a place of malice. They just don't know any better. But regardless of the intentions behind their words, you do not want to leave your peace and sanity to the words of people. Affirmations are words that you speak to charge up your energy and sometimes cancel out the negatives words that people speak towards you. I start my day with the following chant;

"I am a strong powerful component in the universe and I have been empowered to take charge of my day"

Find phrases and positive words that you connect with. Whenever you are feeling overwhelmed by your emotions or the activities going on around you, speak those words and absorb the energy that they give out to you.

Bring Joy into your life

If you have been waiting for that one person whose connection would bring joy into your life, you have been looking in the wrong place. The only person that you need to complete your life is you. You need to stop waiting for some other person's permission to be happy. This is something that you are going to have to deal with by yourself. Empaths are not fond of this truth but trust me, the moment you accept this, you would activate healing in you that is so profound. It would also protect you from falling for just anyone who pops up on your radar. Start doing the things that you love, plan that dream vacation, take that cooking class. Life is too beautiful to spend it waiting. Live your best life now.

Connect with nature

I don't think that there are a lot of things as refreshing as connecting with nature. It revitalizes your soul and leaves you feeling uplifted. A simple walk in the woods can leave you mentally destressed. Surrounding yourself by nature is like entombing yourself in mother earth. This is symbolic of being in the womb which is one of the safest places we have ever known. When you are there, absorb the tranquil energy from what you are surrounded by. If you find yourself by the beach, listen to the sounds of the waves crashing on the shore. Picture your fears and anxiety being broken apart by those waves and let relief wash over you. Accept the blessings and protection energies that you get and believe that you are loved and protected. You would experience a feeling of wholesomeness.

Determine your limits

Empaths struggle with a sense of lack of control. This is the cause of the emotional turmoil that they are always experiencing. It feels as though the world and the events around them happen without their consent. This leaves them in a state of pain, hurt and emotional trauma. To overcome this, it is important to remind yourself daily that everything and anything that happens to you happens with your permission. It is perfectly okay to say no. Put the 'no' out there and let that be your limit. When you feel tired and weary and don't want to go on in terms of dealing with people and their drama, it is okay to say no. Don't let your fear of other people's perception control your reaction. Put your feet down and say no more than you normally would. The essence of this exercise is to empower you and get you to that place where you can embrace the control you have over your life.

Positive Affirmations All Empaths Must Know

With each chapter and segment of this book, I am sure that you got a more intimate knowledge of yourself. Now with that knowledge comes the need to take action. You know what they say, knowledge without action is useless. But before we get to the part where you start acting out the information and wisdom you have received, let us begin that journey by empowering the beautiful person within you. I talked about affirmations before and now we're going to get practical with them. Here are a few affirmations that I feel would be very impactful in the life of an empath

1. I am a beautiful and sensitive soul. My sensitivity is a powerful strength and with this strength, I change my world.

2. I am a very important person, and, in my life, I promise to have people value me as a person. My inner circle is made up of people who value my opinions, my presence, and my feelings.

3. Today I attract blessings and positive energies my way. I reject anything that would infect my world with negativity. My life is beautiful. My experiences are beautiful. My love is beautiful.

4. I have been blessed with the gift to intuitively recognize what is good for me. I listen to my instincts. I trust my instinct and I am protected by my instincts. As long as I listen to my inner voice, I will not come to harm.

5. Today I build a wall around me that protects my energy from people who are emotionally exhausting. I commit myself to staying in relationships that nurture me just as much as I nurture them.

6. I deserve happiness and so today, I will pamper myself. I will treat myself to a healthy diet. I will exercise my mind and body. Today, I am making a commitment to be good to myself.

Chapter Seven - The Healthy, Happy Empath

Now that we have looked at the injured empath as well as the problems that empaths face and then we've gone through this process where we find healing within, how do we know that we have been healed? That is the essence of this chapter. I want us to take a good look at what a happy empath looks like. Because yes, it is possible to be happy and healthy both emotionally and physically. It is always going to take a lot of work. There is no need to hide from that fact. We know that we are built differently than the average person and so the way we react to situations and events in our life is different. Despite the hurdles brought on by our inherent nature, we will find healing. There is no doubt about it but sometimes, the best thing that can motivate you into taking the best course of action for you would be to get a clear vision of yourself. And that is where we are getting to in this chapter. I am not trying to paint a rosy picture. Just in case you haven't noticed, I started this chapter by reiterating some of the difficulties that I feel we would encounter on some level. That said, I think it is time to unveil the person you could become if you stick to the course. Continue in your affirmations and stay healthy both mentally and physically and the result would be rewarding.

The 5 Powerful Lessons Every Empath Must Learn

1. Saying no does not make you a horrible person

When you put an empath in a position with their supposed to say yes or no, instinctively they want to say yes. This is their nature and, in a world, where everything is perfect, this is the right attitude to have. Unfortunately, the world is anything but perfect and so saying yes, every single time you're asked only sets you up for a life of regret. As you evolve on your journey as an empath. This is one of the most critical lessons you would learn. Life does not end when you say no.

As a matter of fact, the opposite is what happens. Your life begins at the end of your no.

2. It is perfectly okay to put yourself first

The empath is generous to a fault. They put the feelings and emotions of others before their own. This nature is what endears them to people but at the same time, it is what destroys them from the inside. On this journey, if you are going to become a better version of yourself, one lesson you must learn is that it is perfectly okay to put yourself first.

3. Your sensitivity is a strength

All your life, you have been told that emotions make a person weak. The fact that you have been sensitive to the things that happen around you has earned you the title of a weak and sensitive person but on this journey, you will discover that your sensitivity is one of your biggest strength. And the more information you acquire about yourself the more powerful you become.

4. You were never the problem

People are going to try and throw your nature in your face. Especially people with whom you have shared some kind of relationships with. Whether it's at work, in school or in your personal relationship. Because of their inability to understand the kind of person you are, it is always going to seem as though you are the problem from the onset. But with the information you get about yourself as you continue to study your personality and understand what empaths are about, you would realize that the problem was never you in the first place. And it is not about allocating the blame. It is about recognizing things for what they really are. Remind yourself constantly (no matter how loud they say otherwise) that the cause of the problem is not you for people's lack of understanding.

5. Happiness is a choice that you make

This here is not something that is unique to just empaths alone a lot of times we fail to realize that the way we feel is actually the only thing that we can control. And yet that is the very thing that we choose to leave in the hands of other people. Happiness is not going to come and knock on your door. It is not going to come in the form of a person who you assume is the perfect one for you. It is not going to be present even if you find that perfect relationship or you suddenly wake up wealthy. Happiness is like waking up every morning and deciding to brush your teeth. It is something that you have to strive for every day and if you take anything away from this particular section of the book, let it be the fact that you are in control of the state of your mind.

Daily Practices of a Healthy Empath

If happiness is something that you have to strive for every day, what then are those things that a happy empath would do to retain their happiness? It is a curious question especially when you consider the fact that happiness means a lot of things to different people. From my personal experience, true happiness does not come from the things that you can own or the things that you can buy. Genuine happiness is found in the little pleasures that you take in the little moments that come to you. It can be very fleeting which is why it is important to be present in every moment because if you miss out on those moments, you wouldn't miss opportunities to be happy. Many of us spend our days procrastinating are happiness. We think that if we are able to get that job if we are able to buy that house; if we finally get to meet that perfect person right now, our lives would be so much better and that is when we know we can finally find happiness. But the thing is that by declaring these words we deprive ourselves of a real shot at happiness. Stop waiting for happiness to happen to you. Use these daily exercises to inject some happiness into your life.

Take a minute to be grateful

One of the reasons that we are unable to find happiness is that we are so focused on the things that we don't have, that we forget about the things that we do have. We place so much value on what we hope to get and pay no attention to the blessings that are already in our lives. No matter how bad a situation is they are little blessings around it. And you can only find those blessings if you make a conscious effort. So, when you wake up in the morning take out a minute of your day to be thankful for all that you have. As they say, you have to develop an attitude of gratitude.

Begin your next adventure

When you get stuck in a rut, your life becomes a very boring place. You lose that sense of wonder which brings some kind of happiness to your life. It is hard to see the good things that you have and appreciate them for what they are and it's not necessarily because you are not thankful. I think it has more to do with the fact that you have lost the lust for life. Today, go on a mini-adventure. It doesn't have to be something grand. It could be something as simple as trying out a new cuisine or maybe starting a new sport. The goal is to bring a sense of newness into your life; to renew your passion for life. When you're passionate about your life, you find happiness in the littlest things.

Show yourself some love

You deserve happiness. I have said this several times and that goes to tell you how important it is. Now showing yourself love is something that many of us kick against instinctively because we think that it creates is a certain perception about us. The fact that we care so much about what other people may think about us more than what we think about ourselves says a lot about our mental state. You don't need to wait for people to love you. As a matter of fact, not many people can love you more than you love yourself. If you want to welcome love into your life, the first place to start from is with you. Show yourself some love. Be kinder to yourself, take out time to pamper yourself. I know they say that going out to eat alone may seem a little depressing. Again, this is the perception of other people. If you want to dine out, I recommend doing it once in a month or so. Take yourself to the finest restaurant you can afford, treat yourself to a lovely meal. Or go to a spa if that is your thing. Enjoy a nice massage. These are little ways you can show yourself, love.

Take a moment to breath

We live very busy lives and the world we are in today moves at a very fast pace. So much so that from the moment you wake up, to the second you put your head down for the day, it seems as though 24 hours just flew by. It is important to take pauses throughout your day. You don't have to do anything significant during those pauses. Something as simple as just focusing on your breathing can do a lot to improve the outcome of your day. When you are feeling tense and wound up, put a pause on whatever it is you are doing. Take a deep breath and exhale; imagine that the tension and stress that you are feeling is flowing out with that breath. There are several breathing exercises that are designed specifically to reduce stress. You could look those up on the internet and maybe try it out. If that sounds a little too complicated for you, just stick to taking pauses during your day. Stop and smell the proverbial roses.

Have a Vision of your future

In very simple terms, this is called dreaming. When you stop dreaming, it is very easy to lose your happiness. That is not to say we should not be rooted in the moment. What I mean is that a vision of your future offers you an alternative that you can walk towards without detaching you from your present. It is important that you recognize the dynamics of this. Going forward, I urge you to dream a little more than you normally would. Picture the happiness that this vision gives you and let it empower your present.

Stop Empathizing with Pain and Start Empathizing with Joy

As empaths, we have a tendency to connect ourselves with pain. When we see someone in pain, we reflect that pain in our lives. This causes us to go through that pain as if it were our own pain. But when it comes to joy or other positive emotions, for some reason we have a detachment. We are unable to reflect that joy and in so doing, we don't live through that joy as if it were our own. Our bias toward pain is not something that is easily understood. Perhaps it is because the pain has an intensity that calls us or maybe the fact that we can be actively involved in resolving some other person's pain. When it comes to joy, on the other hand, it feels as though because there is nothing we can do about it, we don't get involved as much and I think that this is the crux of the problem. When we witness emotions in other people, we are psychologically programmed to react to it and not just react. We want to do something about it.

Well, that was just me speculating, however, science tells us something similar. According to science, our brains do not react with the same intensity to joy as it does to pain. What that means is that as humans, we have an easier time sharing in the pain and suffering of others then we do in sharing their joy. I believe that this experience is even more true for empaths. Experts believe that there is a lot more psychological reward when you are reacting to other people's pain than there is when you react to their joy. This goes on to reinforce my theory that we feel a lot better when we are involved in someone's process and pain allows you more involvement than joy does. When you see a person experiencing joy, you simply have to be happy for that person. But when he comes to pain, our "fixer personality' is put to good use. Now, this does not mean that we want people to be in pain all the time or even at all. It just goes to show what we do subconsciously.

And just because you are programmed to do something subconsciously doesn't mean that your personality has been defined by this. You can take the step to change this attitude. It is good to respond to the pain in other people, but it is also good to respond to their happiness. This is not just for the person you are reacting to but for yourself as well. In order to be a happy, healthy and well-grounded empath, it is important that you strike a balance between these two reactions. When you see someone happy, go ahead and actively rejoice with them. There is no rule that says you cannot do something to celebrate that happiness. If you make the conscious effort to celebrate the happiness of others you would find that there are also rewards involved in this too.

So, today I want you to add to your list of affirmations the desire to celebrate the happiness of other people. When next someone in your circle announces a piece of good news, offer to take them out to celebrate the event. You don't even need to wait until something positive happens. You can just whip out a pen and paper and draft an appreciation letter to your friend, family or loved one the old-fashioned way. Think of a creative way to showcase your empathy for their happiness. It may be a bit of a drag in the beginning, but as you keep at it, it becomes a normal part of you.

Practice Non-Reactive Empathy

Telling an empath to stop reacting to the emotions and energies that they get off other people is like telling them to stop breathing. This is who we are and by now, I am hoping that you have come to that place of acceptance. Now, this segment is about getting you to that place where you don't react to every energy or vibe around you. This can be difficult especially if you're surrounded by people in pain. However, you must bear in mind that to become a happy and healthy empath, this is a skill you are going to have to learn. Look at the things going on around you and develop a different way of reacting to those things. See how I am not telling you to stop reacting? I'm simply saying develop a different form of reaction. To be able to do this, you have to come from a place of self-awareness. Knowing who you are and how certain things make you feel equip you to be more prepared as you can anticipate your reaction.

Another thing you have to understand is that nothing is the way it seems. You may have emotionally walked through that person's shoes but that doesn't mean you have a full picture of what is going on. You see, this is a common mistake that is very peculiar to us as empaths. We feel that our connection to the experience of people gives us access to the whole picture. Let us say, for instance, you stumble across a homeless man on the street. He is holding out his tin cup as usual and asking for any spare change. You immediately react emotionally to his present circumstance and you know how he feels in that moment. But the thing is you only about that specific moment. Bearing this in mind would make it easier for you to develop a different reaction or in the very least reduce your emotional reaction to things.

Scientists tell us that 90% of what we do is based on habit. Therefore, if you want to learn how to develop new ways of doing things, you would have to retrain your brain. To be less reactive, I urge you to consciously take a pause before you react. That pause could make a difference between overreacting and reacting appropriately. One neat trick I had was to pinch myself every time I feel like my emotions are going on overdrive. It acts as a warning signal reminding me to slow down. It took a while for me to get this message but today, I am better for it. I still get affected by the pain that other people feel but I won't dive into everything emotion's first anymore. I feel, I think and then I react.

Chapter Eight - Empathy as a Superpower

Now that we have taken off our rose-tinted glasses, we can see empathy for what it really is. And despite all the challenges and struggles that we go through as empaths, it is safe to say that empathy is a superpower. Empathy is that defining quality that makes us human. The ability to see our fellow human go through life's journey; whether good or bad and have their experiences reflected in our own lives without us having to actually go through those experiences is incredible. As empaths, we set the pace for humanity. We are more than observers in the world's bibliography of anything to do with human experiences. We are participators and, in a way, I would say we are the bookkeepers. It is a cool thing when you think about it. To be that person who witnesses life from the view of the other person. I don't care what people say. They may say that you are too emotional or too reactional or just crazy. We are proud empaths and there is no better time than right now to own the power that comes with the name.

The 7 Natural Gifts that All Empaths Possess

1. Empaths are very creative: The unique perspective given to empaths allow them to see the world in the way that most people don't. This view opens us up to a different dimension of things. In other words, we approach situations from a different angle giving us the unique ability to come up with creative solutions. And even when we are not coming up with innovative solutions, we are very adept at creating exceptional art.

2. Empaths are natural healers: Our connection to the things around us whether people, plants or animals give us a link that makes us natural healers. We have an instinctive understanding of the life energy that flows around us, and we play on this knowledge to provide assistance

to whoever and whatever needs it. Combine this with our biological need to provide care and you have the perfect natural healer.

3. Empaths are alert to dangers in the environment: Thanks again to our connection to the world around us when we enter a room, there something in our subconscious or our being that alerts us immediately we get a sense that there is a threat to our lives in that space. This is not something you can explain. It just happens and it is one of those gifts that we are thankful for.

4. Empaths can spot a lie a mile away: This has got to be my favorite gift as an empath; the ability to spot a lie. It doesn't matter how well-crafted the lie is or how much physical evidence is available to support the lie, the moment an empath encounters a lie, they sense its falseness.

5. Empaths can spot the truth: The same way an empath can spot a lie is the same way they can detect the truth. In our dealings with people, we find them doing their best to mask their true intentions or their true feelings. Our connection to people and our ability to read their energy allows see beneath those layers of pretense and unveil the truth.

6. Empaths get the best experiences: Imagine being able to experience the kaleidoscope of human emotion? That plane of intensity leaves you with a variety of experiences is that not many people would ever have the privilege to experience. The moment we are able to get our feelings under control, we open up the doors to experience life at its best.

7. Empaths are good at reading body language: Communication can either be verbal or nonverbal. Most people are only able to understand communication at a verbal level and even then, their inability to sense the true intentions of people makes it difficult to truly understand the direction of that communication. For empaths, this is hardly a problem. To add to that, they can read the body language of a person to determine what they mean or how they feel

The Best Jobs for Empaths

In my experience, empaths who are self-aware can walk in any field that they put their mind to. It is those who are still struggling with their gifts that find it difficult to function maximally in certain areas. And even then, I feel that this has more to do with their individual personality than their gifts as empaths. Now it is one thing to work in a certain field and it is another thing to thrive in that particular field. For this segment, I am going to focus on career pathways where empath is more likely to utilize their gifts and be successful.

This list is more of a guide so, be careful when applying it to your life. You have to factor in things like your area of specialization, your basic skill sets as well as your talents. Deciding to take a detour into these fields based on your gift as an empath alone is not going to guarantee you the kind of success you desire. The message behind everything I am saying that being an empath would complement the skill sets as well as any other basic requirements for these job roles in their respective industries. With that out of the way, let us explore those job roles.

Psychologist: The empaths ability to listen is one of the things that qualify them for this job. However, it would require an empath who is self-aware to thrive as a psychologist. The reason for this is that empaths in their raw and untrained state tend to react emotionally. Psychologists need a sense of detachment. Even if they can identify with the feelings and emotions that their patient is going through, there still has to be that line for them to be able to offer an objective perspective and as well as creative solutions. Nevertheless, I believe that an empath was born for this job.

Veterinarian: In almost every setting, your local vet is also known as the animal whisperer. They have a way of connecting with the animals under their care and this is not a skill that is learned in any classroom. It is something that is inborn. You need the training in order to provide the right solution, but you need that intuitive ability in order to truly understand the problem.

Artist: It is common knowledge that artists are people with extremely tortured souls and that's because they seem to be sensitive to the world around them. It would make sense to come to this conclusion because it would require you to have a great depth of insight to be able to see things that other people look at as ordinary and transform it into something spectacular. Artists are the reason you can look at a painting and be moved to tears. Or you can listen to a sound and be transported to another universe or you read a set of words and your emotions are stirred. This comes from empathy

Guidance Counselor: This is similar to the psychologist, except this time around, you are helping young people determine their career path and helping kids make the right choices in school. And I feel like this is a role that is very suited to an empath because they can relate to these people like no other person can and also, their intuitive ability to read the true emotions and intentions of people put them in a better position to offer advice when it comes to things like their career or sexual the choices in school among other things.

Lawyer: People without voices need an advocate to speak for them and no person can do this better than someone who is an empath the ability to relate with the situation and the astuteness provided by their training would make them a lethal combination in the courtroom.

How Empaths Can Use Their Gifts to Manifest Success

Empaths are in possession of a lot of gifts that I fell would give them a head start in the workplace their success is not only linked to their career. If applied correctly different areas of your life, you would find yourself thriving. For this segment, I am going to look at five different areas in your life and we would look at how you can use your gift as an empath to get a "leg-up" in that department.

In your career

Regardless of the kind of job that you do, the odds are, you have other people that you work with. For an empath, this gives you the extra advantage because you have an innate understanding of how the relationship dynamics between people work. For you to succeed in the workplace; here is how to work your gifts to your advantage;

1. Use your gift of insight into problems to develop innovative solutions. Your challenge in this regard would be getting your voice heard. Relax, speak your truth and impress your colleagues with your amazing ideas.
2. Use your ability to sense energy to work on timing. This is very helpful when pitching new projects to the boss or lodging a complaint.

In your relationships

For the empath who is yet to understand their personality, their relationships are either complicated or one-sided. With the knowledge you have gained, you can build relationships that are healthy and thrive.

1. Use your gift of separating the truths from the lie, you can actively select the kind of people who you instinctively know to have your best interest at heart. This keeps the energy around you positive
2. Use your creative ability to come up with gift ideas, fun activities and other unique experiences that bond people together and foster friendships

In your finances

Money is tricky for anyone. Empath or not you need basic financial knowledge in order to effectively manage your money. Understandably, money is not a strong motivating force for the empath but there is no reason why you cannot be wealthy. That said, your empathic abilities can help you in the following areas;

1. Monetize your passion. Empaths are moved by the things that they are passionate about. If you can find a way to make your passion a source of income, you would hit a jackpot.
2. Use your network to build net worth. Your relationships are usually your most valuable assets. Grow that and your assets grow.

In your mental health

As much as empaths deal with a lot of emotional problems, if they can also have the best emotional experience. To thrive mentally, do the following;

1. Use your energy radar to filter the kinds of energy you allow into your space. With positive energies, you grow. Negative energies, on the other hand, have a withering effect on you.
2. Use your ability to connect to establish a connection with your true intentions. People walk through life confused about the things that they want. This puts them in a terrible mental state. But not you. Put your mind to it and you can at every point in time know exactly what you want.

In your spiritual life

Your spirituality is not about religion now. But about having harmony in body, mind, and spirit. Empaths are one of the most spiritual beings and you can amplify the experience by doing any of the following

1. Tap into the energy that surrounds nature to revitalize and refresh yourself. This would drain out any of the negative excesses brought into your life and help keep you in a state of bliss
2. Plug your natural talent into your gift of perception. This way, you are connected to a seemingly endless supply of ideas.

People tend to burn out and when they do, they become restless in their quest to regain what they have lost. Your empathic gift can provide a sustainable supply for your talent

The Power of Empathy in the Modern Day

The world that we live in today is chaotic. There is hardly any day that you turn on the news and you would not witness the misery and tragedy that other people are dealing with. The advent of technology has made it possible for media to get to the farthest corners of the earth and bring these tales of woes to your doorstep. With constant exposure to these things, it is not surprising that people have become emotionally detached from the sufferings of people. It has gotten so bad that empathy has become an almost extinct commodity in the human range of emotions.

Today's world is evolving and it is my opinion that without empathy, the world would topple into a chaotic state. Empathy is what creates a balance between the pain that one human is capable of inflicting and the joy that another human is capable of giving. Empathy is what characterizes humanity. We have our differences in experiences, in personalities and in our beliefs. Empathy is the bridge that connects us all. They say that love is a general language and everyone understands it. This was perhaps true a few centuries ago. In the state where the world is right now, love has multiple languages and it takes a level of self-awareness to not just speak it but to speak it fluently.

Empathy is the new universal language. The ability to connect with another being and be interested in their welfare enough to invest in it is what the world needs and this is empathy at the general level. Empathy responds to need and the world is a place that is full of needy people and I don't mean that in the 'clingy' sense. Everyone needs to be heard on some level by someone else. Without empathy, that need would continue to grow for a long time leading to tensions. Today's world is running on the fumes created by these tensions and empathy is the only way to diffuse the situation.

All I am trying to say here is that you are valuable now more than ever. We started this journey with people's perception of empaths. And in retrospect, it would be safe to say that their analogy puts empaths somewhere between an alien and a crazy person. I believe that now you know better. Now you know that you are a sensitive, spiritual being that is full of light and life. The struggles that you have had up to this point are temporary and if you consistently put in the knowledge you have gained here to work, you have the potential to be an extraordinary person. You are the superhero that the world needs in their corner. Your presence is a constant reminder that there is a lot of good in the world and we do not have to look to the skies for angels.

Conclusion

At the start of the book, my goal was to document my journey from being a crazy, out of control empath to this person who is self-aware and rooted in the gifts that I have been given. But with each paragraph, I started picturing your face. As the features of your face became clearer, I started seeing your personality and from your personality, you became a whole person to me. Somewhere along the way, this stopped being my journey. It became our journey and it made me even more excited to share everything that I have learned on my way here with you. People have tried to define us by their own experiences and for the longest time, this has been the yardstick for empaths. We are sensitive, we are emotional, we don't have it together and if like me you imbibed that message, I can imagine how troubled your life must have been up to this point. And this is why I wrote this book. I wanted to reflect the potential that every empath has. We are not reclusive, cry babies but powerful warriors with the ability to change our world. Try that on for size!

We took a lot of detours on this journey and the purpose of it was to look into every aspect of our day to day living. I wanted to break it down into relatable bits. I see this book as a mirror and the clearer it is, the better the vision of yourself that you get. We started off by changing the narrative on who we are and then gradually went into how we deal with everyday situations. We even walked into the dark side of being an empath and to be honest, that was a very difficult process for me. I saw some of the mistakes I have made and that brought back memories of some of the lowest points in my life. I got a very distinct feeling that you had lived through similar pains too. But the good things is that starring into that abyss empowered my decision to be better. Which is why when we moved to the chapters where we talked about our unique abilities. The most intriguing bit for me is the discovery that I actually have the ability to define my life. And this is something that we all share as humans, more so for empaths.

I am hoping that after everything you have read and discovered in this book, that you find the courage to embrace the strength that I know you have on the inside and that you start living your best life now. I can wish from now to the ends of the universe but it is not going to change a thing if you do not believe that you are deserving of this precious gift. Years ago, when I felt that my life was over and I had nothing else to offer, all I wanted was a second chance at life. I wanted a complete do-over. During the years it took me to learn everything I have unloaded in this book; I got my second chance. I just didn't know that 'this' was it. And by 'this', I am referring to the knowledge I had gained over time. My mother used to tell me that knowledge is useless until you put it to action and at first, that was what this information was for me. Until I started making it practical. And so, I am going to pass on that bit of elderly wisdom across to you. Take everything that you have gained from reading this book and apply it. It is in applying it that you would discover what works for you and what doesn't. As you sieve through that process, you become better, wiser and stronger.

This book outlines the process of getting you to a happier and healthier place step by step. I ensured that content is positive, relatable and practical. Being an empath is not an alien concept. This is our reality and part of my objective was to write a book with a balanced perspective on every aspect of our lives. If I wanted to be dramatic, I would say that this book was about tipping the odds in your favor and I believe that we were able to achieve this. In your hands right now a tool that shows your strengths and weaknesses. It highlights your interests and your passions and it clearly outlines your risks and your rewards. It is not a magician's wand that you can simply flick your wrists, say the magic word and transform your life overnight but it puts the power of transformation in your hands.

And now that we have come to the end, it is my earnest desire that your process does not end the second that you close this book. I want the words that are contained in this book to come alive in your heart. I want them to inspire you in moments when you feel down and activate a passion in you that sees you pursuing your dreams to the fullest. However, as an empath, I understand what your biggest struggle in all of this is going to be and with that knowledge, here is my wish for you. I wish that you would see yourself for the wonderful person that you are and ultimately accept this gift that has been given to you. I can almost see the gears in your brain working in unison and I hope that they steer you towards that space where you can finally accept that you are deserving of happiness. That you no longer need to keep putting your needs and your dreams on the back burner for everyone else. You have just as much right as everyone else to be happy. That is not to say that I want you to stop being you…just a friendly reminder that your dreams and aspirations are a part of who you are. On that note, I say welcome to the best days of the rest of your life. Keep being authentic.

THE MAGIC PRINCIPLES OF THE ENNEAGRAM

Discover Who You Really Are, Your True Needs and Those of Others by Understanding the 9 Personality Types and The Power of The Enneagram

Table of Contents

Introduction **95**

Chapter One - Understanding the Enneagram **98**
What the Enneagram Figure Means 98
How to Identify Your Personality Type 102
About the Levels 103

Chapter Two - The Reformer (Type 1) **106**
Fifteen Signs You're a Reformer 106
The Reformer: An Overview 107
The Reformer Levels 108
The Reformer Wings 113
Advice For The Reformer 116

Chapter Three – The Helper (Type 2) **118**
Fifteen Signs You're a Helper 118
The Helper: An Overview 119
The Helper Levels 120
The Helper Wings 123
Advice for the Helper 125

Chapter Four – The Achiever (Type 3) **127**
Fifteen Signs You're an Achiever 127
The Achiever: An Overview 128
The Achiever Levels 129
The Achiever Wings 132
Advice for the Achiever 135

Chapter Five - The Individualist (Type 4) **136**
Fifteen Signs You're An Individualist 136
The Individualist Overview 137
The Individualist Levels 139
The Individualist Wings 142
Advice for The individualist 144

Chapter Six - The Investigator (Type 5) **146**
Fifteen Signs You're An Investigator 146

The Inspector Overview 147
The Investigator Levels 149
The Investigator Wings 151
Advice for The Investigator.. 153

Chapter Seven - The Loyalist (Type 6).. **155**
Fifteen Signs You're A Loyalist... 155
The Loyalist Overview 157
The Loyalist Levels 158
The Loyalist Wings 161
Advice for The Loyalist.. 163

Chapter Eight - The Enthusiast (Type 7)..................................... **165**
Fifteen Signs You're an Enthusiast 165
The Enthusiast Overview 166
The Enthusiast Levels... 168
The Enthusiast Wings... 170
Advice for The Enthusiast 175

Chapter Nine - The Challenger (Type 8)..................................... **177**
Fifteen Signs You're a Challenger 177
The Challenger Overview... 179
The Challenger Levels 180
The Challenger Wings 183
Advice for The Challenger 186

Chapter Ten - The Peacemaker (Type 9) **188**
Fifteen Signs You're a Peacemaker 188
The Peacemaker Overview 189
The Peacemaker Levels 192
The Peacemaker Wings 195
Advice for The Peacemaker 198

Conclusion **199**

Introduction

The world in which we live is a complex place, teeming with so many different voices, influences and ideas. It can be somewhat of a challenge to remain centered and stay true to who you are, to actually know and understand who you truly are, and take appropriate action based on this vital self-knowledge.

Do you seek clarity in a world that can often feel confusing? Would you like to grow personally, with the confidence that you are growing in the right direction? Perhaps you seek a better understanding of your loved ones. A way to avoid conflict and to achieve more harmony. To learn which partners you are compatible with and to deepen those relationships. If so, the Enneagram might well provide the solution you have been seeking.

Modern theories relating to the Enneagram are variously credited to the teachings of George Gurdjieff, Oscar Ichazo and Claudio Naranjo. It is a system of nine different personality types and it combines the considerable benefits of both modern psychology and traditional wisdom. It can be used as a powerful tool for understanding ourselves and others. It has also been used extensively in the realms of both spirituality and business - specifically in the areas of team building, leadership development and communication skills.

In this book, you will learn the basic tenets and principles of the Enneagram and receive thorough and revealing outlines of each individual personality type. You will discover your own particular 'type' along the way - there are nine in all - and the various strengths and challenges that accompany this. You will come to understand how to use these strengths to your advantage and how to overcome and transcend the unique issues that your particular type might have to grapple with.

Enneagram

For all of my life, I've held a deep passion for self-development and personality tests. It goes beyond everyday interest; my life has truly been shaped by my discoveries. And my deep understanding of the Enneagram has allowed me to read people in a way that most people cannot. By identifying my personality type, I finally became able to identify my true needs. If you don't know what your needs are, how can you ever hope to meet them?

I have discovered from personal experience that by digging deep and learning who I truly am, my life is richer and more meaningful. I am also capable of making much better decisions when it comes to the more important things in life. I am an Enneagram Type Four and this knowledge helps me to know my frailties, to nimbly walk around them and to capitalize on and give myself credit for my strengths. In a way, it makes it easier when I know there is a reason for it all. It is not my fault, it is because I am a Four!

This book can be used as a guide along your road to self-discovery. You can use it as a tool to understand yourself more deeply and to identify your dominant traits. It provides everything you need to know on how to deal with all your wonderful idiosyncrasies and to achieve personal growth along the way. The book can provide additional insight too. By identifying the 'types' of our significant others - be they friends, partners or family members - we achieve a better insight into how to make these relationships work and furthermore, how to deepen them. Communication can be improved and conflicts lessened.

People from all over the world and from every generation have given testimonials about the positive impact of the Enneagram on their lives. This can manifest in a whole range of ways. Examples include recognizing the mental patterns that underlie emotions. Developing self-awareness such as learning about the meaning of bodily sensations like tension. Understanding the strategies we use for self-preservation. Owning your own emotions and establishing boundaries. Allowing vulnerability and accessing your own innate wisdom.

Enneagram

This book provides a definitive guide to all you need to know about the Enneagram and how to utilize the knowledge it provides. You will discover your type. Learn your potential strengths and weaknesses. Gain access to the power of self-understanding. You will have a deeper analysis and insight into who you really are and into the personalities of all of those around you. Imagine how useful it would be to gain insight into your prickly co-worker or your difficult boss! And in your romantic life: picture the advantage you will have in assessing potential partners and even avoiding repeating unhealthy relationship patterns from your past.

Life is short. Why waste time in confusion when clarity can be yours? The Enneagram and the insights it reveals can be an excellent place to start. It is said that an unexamined life is not worth living. The Enneagram can provide the awareness that is ultimately the key to all change and leads to far reaching benefits.

Unconscious behaviours and triggers are brought to the fore, enabling us to finally deal with them. Not only can you grow personally, but you can improve your relationships, both in the workplace and with friends and loved ones.

The information pertaining to the Enneagram that is contained in this book has led to life changing and far reaching positive consequences for many. Join the growing ranks of people who have experienced wonderful changes in their friendships, careers, romantic relationships and personal development.

Two thousand years ago, as pilgrims approached the sacred temple at Delphi, they were greeted by the sign: "Know Thyself." This sage advice is just as relevant today. Self-knowledge is power. But first you have to seek it. Then use it. This book can help you do just that.

Chapter One - Understanding the Enneagram

There are many personality tests in the public domain. You may have heard of some of them. The Myers Briggs personality test is one of the most famous of these, and you might have taken this yourself. But I would venture to say that The Enneagram is more than a personality test. It would be more accurately described as an immensely powerful tool for personal, not to mention collective, transformation.

So just what is this enigma known as the Enneagram? To delve a little deeper into its true meaning and origins, we are first going to examine the symbol which represents it.

What the Enneagram Figure Means

The Enneagram symbol or figure is made up of three individual shapes, each having its own separate meaning. We will first examine the underlying circle:

The Circle

It will come as no surprise that the circle represents the wholeness or oneness of life - as in the Circle of Life. The circle also serves as a kind of container within which we conduct our lives. As we navigate our way through life, fragmentation can occur, often because of the ego. The goal is to reach awareness that we have never actually lost our wholeness.

The Triangle

In many cultures, three is regarded as a mystical and magical number. This is sometimes known as the Law of Threes. This law holds that every phenomenon consists of three individual forces. When three forces are present, things start to happen. But with only one or two forces available, nothing at all happens. Each force has a different name. The first is known as the active or positive or motivating force. The second one is called the negative or passive or denying force and the third is named the neutralizing, facilitating or invisible force. As an esoteric law, the Law of Threes works both in our inner world and our outer world. You might be able to observe it in your interactions with other people.

There are numerous cultural examples of the Law of Threes. One of the most pervasive and one which the majority of people will be familiar with, is that of the concept of the holy trinity - the father, son and The Holy Spirit - which is espoused by the Christian tradition.

The Hexad

The Hexad is a more unusual and irregular symbol which finds its origins in Sufism - the mystical branch of Islam. It is actually a six pointed figure but it follows seven points, from the start, through six changes of momentum, then back to its origin, which is considered the seventh point. It represents the Law of Seven, which is sometimes known as the law of octaves. It propounds that phenomena evolves in seven steps. Along with the Law of Threes, it was believed by Gurdjieff, a chief proponent of The Enneagram, that the Law of Seven was a global law and essential to his cosmology.

The Law of Seven states that the path of movement, either towards or away from anything, does not occur in a straight line. Rather, there are periods of striving, falling and striving again - a kind of rising and falling of energies along the way.

These three shapes are overlaid onto one another in order to create the Enneagram symbol. The lines on the Enneagram symbol show a path to a richer and fuller life. Self-observation is encouraged here, in order to avoid the different triggers of our personalities which might tend to lead one astray.

Enneagram

The numbers - one to nine - on the Enneagram symbol, represent the nine different personality types. The relationship between the numbers are demonstrated by the lines that connect them together. Each number is only connected to two other numbers.

About the Wings

No one person is made up purely of one personality type. Everyone is a mixture of their main type together with one of the two types next to it on the Enneagram figure. Whichever adjacent type that you most identify with is known as your 'wing.'

Your dominant wing is indicated by the higher score of one of the types that exists on either side of your basic type. For example, if your basic type is Three, your wing will be Two or Four, whichever one has the highest score. It is worth noting that the second highest overall score on your Enneagram test is not necessarily that of your wing.

The idea is that the wing types have an extra influence on your basic type.

The Triads (or Centers)

The nine personality types of the Enneagram are arranged into three triads, otherwise known as centers. Three of the types are in the instinctive center (One, Eight and Nine), three in the feeling center (Two, Three and Four) and three in the thinking center, (Five, Six and Seven). The three personalities that occupy the same center share the same strengths and weaknesses as one another.

Enneagram

Each triad or center is associated with a particular emotion. The instinctive center is associated with anger, whereas the feeling center tends to feel more shame. And the thinking center is linked to feelings of fear. Of course, each and every person can be subject to each and every emotion, but in each triad, the personalities associated with it are especially affected by that triad's emotional theme. You'll find that each personality type has a particular way of coping with its dominant emotion.

The three numbers within each triad or center have a pattern that they follow. The first number in each triad *expresses* the emotion that it is hyper-focused on. So types Eight, Two and Five express and externalize their emotions. This means that Eight externalizes anger, Two externalizes shame and Five externalizes fear.

This means that they either project the emotion outwardly or experience it outside themselves. When these personalities experience these emotions, they manifest right in front of us.

The second number in each center *represses* the emotion upon which it focuses. That is, Nine, Three and Six. So Nine represses anger, Three represses shame and Six represses fear. In other words, they do their best to pretend that the emotion doesn't exist for them.

The third number in each center *internalizes* the emotion it is most associated with. Thus, One, Four and Seven try to internalize their emotions. One internalizes anger, Four internalizes shame and Seven internalizes fear. These personalities experience these emotions inwardly or turn it in on themselves. This is different from repression because they still feel the emotion they are concealing, but they are choosing not to show it. This may lead these personality types, especially Four, to brood.

How to Identify Your Personality Type

The upcoming chapters provide a comprehensive guide to the nine different personality types, set out in numerical order. Each chapter begins with a check list comprising of fifteen questions to ask yourself in order to ascertain whether or not you are likely to be that particular type.

It would be a good idea to keep a record of which personality type you tick off the most statements for. This practice should identify your personality type. In a similar way, keep track of which adjacent personality type you score the most for. This will be your dominant wing.

It is quite common to find a little of yourself in all of the nine Enneagram personality types, although one of them should stand out as being the closest to you. This is your basic type.

We are all familiar with the ongoing debate between nature and nurture. In terms of the Enneagram, experts agree that we are born with a dominant type. This inborn temperament seems to determine the ways in which we adapt to our early childhood environment.

People do not switch from one personality type to another. For instance, if you are born a One, you will stay a One for the entirety of your life. A few other points are worth bearing in mind. All the types apply equally to men and to women. And a larger number on the Enneagram scale is no better or worse than a lower number. In other words, an eight is no better than a three or vice versa. Each type has its own inherent strengths and weaknesses. No Enneagram personality type is better or worse than another. We should all strive to be our best selves rather than striving to emulate other types.

About the Levels

Of course, not all the people from the same type will be exactly the same. This is obvious when we consider the diversity of the human beings we are surrounded with. So what is it that accounts for these differences?

Each personality type is made up of nine levels of development. This hypothesis was first reached by Don Riso in 1977. Riso, together with Russ Hudson, further developed the idea in the 1990s. The concept of the levels adds depth to our understanding of the Enneagram system and accounts both for the differences that arise between people of the same type and also how people can change, positively or negatively.

The levels of development provide deeper understanding to the explanation of the different elements contained within a personality type. This ties in with the complexity of human nature. The levels of development provide for us a kind of skeletal framework which allows us to see how all the traits of a particular type are interrelated, and how a healthy trait can become average, or can become unhealthy. Of course, this can work in the opposite direction also.

The levels show us that the personality is dynamic and ever changing. It helps us understand that people can change states within their personality, shifting within the spectrum of traits that make up their personality type.

It can help significantly in our understanding of others to assess whether someone is in their healthy, average or unhealthy level of functioning.

The nine levels of development are comprised of three levels in the healthy segment, three levels in the average segment and three levels in the unhealthy segment. Shades of grey abound.

Enneagram

The continuum of the levels of development is as follows:

Healthy

Level 1: The level of liberation

Level 2: The level of psychological capacity

Level 3: The level of social value

Average

Level 4: The level of imbalance/social role

Level 5: The level of interpersonal control

Level 6: The level of overcompensation

Unhealthy

Level 7: The level of violation

Level 8: The level of obsession and compulsion

Level 9: The level of pathological destructiveness

Try and be as honest as you can when it comes to assessing your own level. Even though this can sometimes expose uncomfortable truths, it is the surest path to personal growth.

Levels can be understood in terms of our capacity to be present. The further we move down the levels, the less present we are and the more we are identified with the ego and its negative patterns. The lower down the levels we go, the more defensive, compulsive and destructive we become. We tend to be less free, less self-aware, and act on a more sub-conscious level.

Conversely, as we move up the levels, we become more and more present. We are less destructive and increasingly free and open. We are far more self-aware and astute. We are less likely to get caught up in negativity.

Becoming more present allows us to be more objective about our personality and we become adept at self-observation. This makes us more effective in all areas of our lives, whether that be relationships or our career. It can bring genuine peace and joy to whatever it is that we are doing.

Chapter Two - The Reformer (Type 1)

Also known as the Perfectionist

Fifteen Signs You're a Reformer

1. You strive to make the world a better place in which to live. You are capable of seeing, in clear detail, what is wrong with a situation and you are prepared to take the necessary steps to rectify matters.

2. You possess a very strong sense that you have a life purpose or a mission to fulfill.

3. Other people often describe you as being responsible, dependable and brimming over with common sense. They can also sometimes accuse you of having no feelings. (You *do* have feelings – you're just keeping them all in!)

4. You think you have to do everything perfectly, going so far as to think that *you* yourself have to be perfect.

5. You are highly self-disciplined - sometimes to a fault. You have little to no trouble sticking to a schedule or routine.

6. You hate feeling stagnant and you always ache to be useful in some way.

7. You feel you have to keep a lid on all your very strong wants and needs.

8. It is vitally important to you that you 'do the right thing.'

9. You have an intense fear of making mistakes or blunders.

10. You tend to experience tension in your shoulders, neck and jaw.

11. It sometimes takes you longer than the average person to complete a task, which is, of course, because of your exceptional eye for detail.

12. You can be very critical of yourself and others.

13. You may experience disappointment and frustration at those times when reality does not meet your expectations.

14. You hold yourself to very high standards of excellence.

Does this sound anything like you?

The Reformer: An Overview

Perfectionism can be a double-edged sword. On the one hand, it can cause impressive and wonderfully satisfying results. On the other, it can lead to wounding self-criticism and even inaction, where the perfectionist might not even begin a task for fear of failure.

Type One in The Enneagram model is not lacking in the least when it comes to admirable traits such as reliability, honesty, common sense, integrity and nobility. In fact, this type can be downright heroic. They could, however, learn to be kinder to themselves. Although lowering your standards is not usually to be recommended, Ones could sometimes benefit from taking such advice, as the expectations they heap upon themselves - and others - can be unrealistically and punishingly high.

This type wishes to make the world a better place, and what's not to like about that?! High ideals are the order of the day, coupled with a strong sense of purpose. These people get things done and done right!

You might also recognize a One by their fastidious attention to detail: that go-to co-worker who you can always rely on. Granted, they may take longer than most to complete the task, but the end result will be undoubtedly flawless. Or it might be the friend with the incredible self-discipline, who will keep to the diet or the exercise regime and whose gym membership will be used beyond the third week in January.

If you want to keep in a One's good books, make sure you keep your promises. *Never* say you are going to do something and then back out or forget about it. This is a complete no-no and breaks their ethical code. These good people would never do the same to you! And don't forget to take things seriously. This type does not appreciate a flippant attitude. It will surprise and delight them if you join them in speculating about how things can be improved in the world, and you will make all their dreams come true by actually taking action. Encourage them also to be less critical of themselves. Teach them that a little self-kindness goes a long way. Above all, a One needs a friend who can coax them to have fun and to take life - and themselves - a little less seriously.

The Reformer Levels

Healthy

Heroism

Type Ones on The Enneagram are the stuff that heroes are made of. A man by the name of Gandhi comes to mind. He embodied the qualities of the One at his or her best, in his capacity for extraordinary wisdom and discernment. His humanity inspired immense loyalty and made him a great leader that thousands of people felt compelled to follow. And we need look no further than Joan of Arc for a historical example of a One who uplifted many and created change through the courage of her conviction and willingness to self sacrifice.

Not every One can be a Gandhi or a Joan of Arc, but within their own private sphere of influence, no matter how big or small, they can often perform acts of everyday heroism.

Practical Action

It is one thing to have lofty ideals. It is quite another to act in accordance with them. But the One is a master of practical action, striving always to be useful, to fix the things that they consider broken and to fulfil their powerful mission in life. These people put their money where their mouth is. They have no qualms around making personal sacrifices to serve a higher cause.

Loyalty

The Reformer will not say one thing and then do another. They are impeccable with their word. Neither will they make promises to do something and then not do it. If you are lucky enough to have the friendship of a One, you know that you have someone who will always have your back.

Attention to Detail

Enneagram

A One will not leave a job half-done. Neither will they turn in a shoddy project. They always strive for excellence, in thought, word and deed. This type is always pushing the envelope and raising standards - for themselves and the world in which they live. Consider these prominent Ones in the areas of politics, business and entertainment. Such people as: Nelson Mandela, Michelle Obama, Anita Roddick (The Body Shop), Martha Stewart, Dame Maggie Smith and Meryl Streep, Confucious, Margaret Thatcher, Plato, George Bernard Shaw, Noam Chomsky, Emma Thompson, Jane Fonda, Jerry Seinfeld, George Harrison, Hilary Clinton, Jimmy Carter, Prince Charles.

Integrity

A One's deep sense of integrity makes him or her an excellent teacher and, in general, a witness and proponent of the truth. They are principled to the core and will uphold these principles even at the cost of their own safety or comfort. You can trust them to always do the right thing, even if this goes against conventional wisdom or public opinion. The Reformer will not be swayed from what he or she believes to be right and good.

Neutral or Average

Dissatisfaction

The Reformer at this level thinks it is up to them to fix everything. They feel they know how everything 'should' be done and that it is their absolute duty to tell everybody else what they should do too!

Rigidity

This rigidity is caused by the fear of making a mistake. Everything has to be exactly right. There is no margin for error whatsoever, either for the Reformer themselves or for those around them.

Overly critical

The Reformer directs this criticism - not just at him or herself - but at others too. They feel the need to correct people constantly, and not in an especially sensitive way! Very low level of satisfaction.

Unhealthy

Hell is other people!

It's not always easy being a Reformer. You will constantly encounter those with different value systems to your own and this might well upset your high-minded ideals and insistence on excellence. It may lead you to be self-righteous, intolerant, dogmatic or inflexible. You might severely judge others for their inability to see things in the same way that you do.

Obsession

There is a risk that Ones can become obsessive in nature. This can manifest itself in a number of ways. One of these is in the area of diet and nutrition. In extreme cases, the Reformer's quest for self-control might lead to conditions such as anorexia and bulimia. Some might also resort to alcohol in order to alleviate the stress that they put themselves under. Obsessive Compulsive Disorder is also a danger to this type.

Anger

The Reformer can get angry very easily and this anger can often have a tinge of self-righteousness to it. Offense may be taken easily, from other people's refusal to do what the One believes to be right. This anger - however righteous - can unfortunately have the effect of alienating others. This is a great pity, as Ones often have a very valid point to make. Repressing this anger is not the answer either, as this might manifest in health issues such as high blood pressure or ulcers.

Depression

This is a fate that can befall a person with a dominant Type One personality, when the trait takes an unhealthy turn. A less than healthy Reformer can be extremely condemnatory, not to mention cruel, to themselves and others. Depressions, breakdowns and suicide attempts are the worst possible outcome here.

Unrealistically High Standards

Enneagram Type Ones can struggle with intense disappointment when reality does not match up to their expectations. It can make them appear overly negative or critical of other family members, friends or co-workers. It can make them very harsh task masters - pedantic and unforgiving. It is not pleasant to be on the receiving end of an unhealthy One's constant criticism and disappointment at your efforts.

But it's not all doom and gloom!

So, if you are a One - a Perfectionist, a Reformer - how can you best avoid the potential pitfalls and instead bring out the best in what your personality type has to offer?

The Reformer Wings

Type One with a Two wing (1W2)

What do you get when you cross a Type One with a Type Two? Well, for a start, the One becomes less repressed and a little more emotionally balanced by the two's directedness and desire to please others.

This is often a very neat and tidy-looking person. The One gives them a propensity for perfectionism and the Two makes them more sensitive to criticism. In other words, they don't want to be criticized about their appearance. So their hair will be perfect and clothing will be just so. They might hold themselves very correctly and come across as having rather a condescending attitude.

This subtype is very hard on his or herself. They will make every effort to do the right thing and if they can also manage to please others in the process, that's even more preferable.

The healthy version of a One with a Two wing is a more relaxed version of a full One with less of an inclination to be righteously judgmental. They can actually believe and admit that they might not always be right!

The One enjoys correcting others. With the influence of the Two, the corrections become more helpful and less intrusive. They are also better able to tolerate differences with the benefit of the Two wing.

If the Reformer with the Two wing happens to experience a kind of spiritual awakening, he or she can become a most inspiring teacher who can bring joy and compassion to their practice. One is wise and Two is loving. At their best, this sub type can be a sterling friend who always seems to know the right thing to say or do.

But oh dear! Things can take a turn for the worse when the Reformer's not so emotionally healthy and mature. The One's perfectionism combined with the Two's pride can lead to trouble. It can amount to great inner conflict. Self-critical introspection goes into overdrive and may be accompanied by fits of rage which descend into self-judgement and remorse.

When severely unhealthy, the anger and pride combine to create despair. Here, the One with a Two wing will punish themselves endlessly and suicide might even be the end result.

It is not surprising the Reformer with a Two wing might enjoy work that involves helping other people become perfect. Examples of such would be teachers, dieticians and judges.

Type One with a Nine wing (1W9)

The combination of the perfectionism and judgement of Type One with the withdrawal from stress of Type Nine makes for a quiet, conservative and somewhat repressed sub type. They do not show a lot of emotion and they will come across as quite strict, quiet and practical. They are slow to express their views also but will usually act from principled judgement.

They can, of course, shine when emotionally healthy and mature. Here, they will learn to access an inner warmth and be capable of bringing it to the fore. Although they might still be a little judgmental, they allow for the fact that they are capable of getting it wrong at times. And anyway, it doesn't really matter that much after all. They learn at this stage to control the propensity of the Nine to withdraw under stress and this allows them to participate in life more fully. They are gentle, responsible, fun-loving and capable of relaxing and just letting go.

At their very best, they will be ever more joyful and participate in life with much gusto. They will have high self-esteem at this level. The wisdom of the One will merge with the selflessness of the Nine and can allow them to obtain significant spiritual advancement.

But this sub type can be unhealthy too and when they are, they might try to exert too much control over their emotions which will lend to them a physical rigidity punctuated by fissions of explosive energy.

Repressed emotions are ever present under the surface and they will come across as "nervy" types. They will be hostile and withdrawn and suffer from self-hatred. They might be highly suspicious and engage in passive-aggressive behaviour. Most of this will be bottled up.

If things disintegrate even further, they can come across as robotic and ritualistic. Anxiety about performing routines just right can become extreme. They may descend into psychosis and become paralyzed with inaction.

This variant of the One stands upright and offers few, but genuine, smiles. It is possible that they are drawn to work that expresses their talent for performing precise tasks, such as accountancy or computer programming.

Advice For The Reformer

I know you didn't ask for advice, but we're going to give it to you anyway! As a Reformer, you probably don't feel you need any counsel, because of your higher than average sense of right and wrong and your intense feeling of purpose. And you are right, to a point. We each need to follow our own star. However, we all have our weaknesses too, and it can be very useful at times to have a second eye, as it were, to give us a greater sense of perspective.

1. Keep in mind that not everyone will see the world in such black and white terms as you do. There are numerous shades of grey and sometimes you need to make allowances for middle-ground.

2. Find a healthy way to express and release your anger, one that doesn't involve another human having to feel the full extent of your wrath but at the same time, means you don't repress it all, which could lead to serious health problems for you. It may also help to find less reasons to be angry. Accepting other people's imperfections, perhaps! Don't forget that people can be chaotic. If someone turns up late for an appointment, it doesn't necessarily mean that they disrespect you or don't value your time. They might just be struggling with the messiness of their own lives. Be less critical of others. And while you're at it, be less critical of yourself too!

3. Keep in mind the famous serenity prayer: Grant me the serenity to accept the things I cannot change, the courage to change the things I can and the wisdom to know the difference.

4. Be cognizant that you have a tendency to store tension in your body, particularly in your jawline, neck and shoulders. Consider taking steps to counteract this, such as meditation, massage or other relaxation techniques. And why not try to have fun! This is a proven and excellent path to relaxation. After all, nobody likes a martyr!

5. It is possible that you had parents with very high expectations of you. If this is the case, perhaps it is now time to re-parent yourself and show yourself more softness and kindness. Remember: 'Angels fly because they take themselves lightly.' You don't have to take yourself so seriously all the time. And remind yourself often that everyone makes mistakes, including you. You are not a failure if you make a mistake. This is how we learn. Acceptance of this is key. Furthermore, it is perfectly acceptable to have human emotions and impulses. And sometimes 'good enough' is good enough. Perfection is an illusion. So forgive yourself for your imperfections. Forgiveness is a gift to yourself even more so than to the one that you are forgiving.

6. You often feel that the weight of the world is on your shoulders. Thankfully, it is not. You are just one person and you are doing just fine.

7. Trust your inner guidance and most of all, trust life.. Your tendency to see so clearly where things need to be improved, can make you blind to the many things that are right with the world. If you look more closely, you will recognize that things are often working out.

8. Try not to be too disappointed or impatient if those around you don't change immediately in accordance with what you might have taught them. It does not mean that you are not a gifted teacher, but rather that everyone develops at their own pace. Patience is a virtue!

Above all, don't stop being who you are. There is a reason you were born this way so find out why and make the most of it!

Chapter Three – The Helper (Type 2)

Also known as the Giver

Fifteen Signs You're a Helper

1. You love to be involved in other people's lives.

2. You always feel the urge to put other people before yourself.

3. You tend to give a lot of time and money to charity.

4. You are able to see the good in your fellow humans.

5. You need to be needed.

6. You can totally exhaust yourself, running around doing things for other people.

7. You may feel offended if someone refuses your offer of help.

8. You require appreciation for the things you do for others.

9. Your friends describe you as being someone who is always willing to go that extra mile.

10. You sometimes forget to look after yourself and this can lead to physical or emotional burnout.

11. You don't consider life worth living unless you are giving to others in some way.

12. You have a deep seated fear of worthlessness.

13. You might well be a wonderful cook and homemaker!

14. You might have a tendency to use food to 'stuff' down your feelings.

15. Personal relationships are of the utmost importance to you.

Do any of the above points ring a bell?

The Helper: An Overview

The focus of Type Two of the Enneagram is very much on relationships. It is what makes these people tick - making connections and then empathizing with the feelings and needs of others. However, they can go too far in this tendency and can twist themselves into all sorts of shapes just to win approval from their peers. Co-dependency is a trap that type two can sometimes fall prey to, priding themselves on what they can do for other people and feeling shame at those times when they can't actually help or support others.

In a way, our culture nurtures and awards the typical behavior of a Type Two, in that it encourages us to believe that our self-worth comes from what we do for other people. Women especially are taught this kind of behaviour. Although being kind to others is, of course, laudable, the Helper must guard against a tendency to smother or overwhelm. And it is never good for someone to deny their own personal interests and needs. Burnout or martyrdom may ensue! So if you are a Two, you would do well to balance your impulse to assist others with your own self-care.

As a Helper, love is your highest goal. You pride yourself on selflessness. You are often extroverted and may also have the knack for creating a comfortable and welcoming home for your family. You are huge on empathy and often a genuinely caring person with a very warm heart. You are friendly and generous. Just make sure that your motives for helping others are pure.

Examples of famous twos include such luminaries as Bishop Desmond Tutu, Byron Katie, John Denver, Dolly Parton, Eleanor Roosevelt, Luciano Pavarotti, Stevie Wonder, Elizabeth Taylor, Martin Sheen, Bobby McFerrin, Lionel Richie, Nancy Reagan, Josh Groban, Paula Abdul and Barry Manilow.

Type two has been given the name 'The Helper' for a reason: these people are either the most genuinely helpful to others *or* the most in need to see themselves as helpful.

The Helper Levels

As with every other type, Helpers differ in maturity and psychological health. We will explore the state of The Helper at healthy, neutral and unhealthy stages.

Healthy

Unconditionally Loving

The Helper at his or her best is capable of giving truly unconditional love. He or she is humble and unselfish, feeling it is a privilege to give and to be meaningfully involved in the lives of others.

Empathetic

Empathy is the helper's middle name. This type can be spilling over with compassion and concern for their fellow human beings. In addition, they have learnt the art and value of forgiveness.

Encouraging

The Helper at this level can easily appreciate the goodness of other people. They have learnt to balance service with self-care and give for all the right reasons.

Neutral

The People-Pleaser

An air of desperation can sometimes creep into Type Two's desire to help others. A kind of clinging rather than closeness. They might be tempted to give compliments that are not entirely genuine but instead meant to gain favor from the person they are flattering.

The Co-Dependent

This stage involves possessiveness and intrusiveness. The need to be needed can become so strong that the Type Two can be deeply controlling yet tell themselves that they are actually being loving. They want others to be dependent on them and often wear themselves out with needlessly self-sacrificial behaviour.

Self-Importance

A heightened sense of self-importance is probable at this level. Martyrdom can really kick in with the Helper believing that they are being far more helpful than they actually are! Type Two at this level might feel that he or she is indispensable when they are really not, and this can cause them to be patronizing and overbearing.

Unhealthy

Manipulation

Oh dear! Things start to get nasty when Type Twos exhibit unhealthy behavior patterns. At this level, a Two may well pile on the guilt, highlighting how much they believe people owe them for all they've done. This level displays the general attitude of "How *could* you after everything I've done for you?!" If people do not show the requisite level of appreciation, they might undermine them in an aggressive way. At this level, the Two will lack the self-awareness to see how unreasonable and damaging their behavior is. They may also begin to use food and drugs as a way of self-medication.

Domineering

At this unsavory level, the Two feels that everybody they've "helped" - whether or not that person asked for that help in the first place or actually wanted it at all! - owes them an enormous debt of gratitude and therefore must "pay" in whatever way the Two deems appropriate. There is a negative sense of entitlement where this type asserts the hold they feel they have earned.

Chronic Resentment

Such resentment arises when an unhealthy Two steps fully into victim mode and feels unjustly abused by those they have "helped." Because of this, they feel justified in displaying all sorts of irrational and aggressive behavior. All these highly negative emotions can result in serious health problems, both physical and mental. Not a happy place to be! Both for the Helper and for those around them.

The Helper Wings

As previously discussed, a type's wings are derived from the two number types that are physically beside it on the circumference of the Enneagram figure. For the Helper, the Reformer (Type 1) and the Achiever (Type 3) are possible wings or influencers on the personality.

Type Two with a One Wing (2W1)

We have already seen that Type Ones are perfectionists at heart. On the plus side, they are responsible, conscientious, progress-oriented and potentially heroic. Their shadow side can be hyper-critical, this being directed both at themselves and others. At times, they can also be resentful and judgemental. So what can a Type Two with a One wing look like?

All going well, this combination of types leads to a person who is loving, warm and generous, as you would expect, but the One influence adds resolve and moral obligation. The desire to do good is thus heightened by the number One's motivation to do everything 'right.'

The focus of the One's generosity becomes a drive for social justice under the influence of the Reformer. The desire to improve the world is genuine. The Helper with this wing is also more willing to take on the unglamorous tasks that other people usually eschew, for the sake of the common good. The influence of the One on the Two can imbue them with a stronger backbone and a better awareness of where feelings might threaten to overtake their good judgment.

But, as always, there is a flip side. Destructive perfectionism could rear its ugly head, causing the helper to think that they, and they alone, know best. This makes them imposing, preachy and intrusive. They may also judge themselves very severely. A potential negative side of this combination of types can also be that the Two has even more trouble recognizing her own needs and feelings and strongly believes that her own personal desire is selfish and should be quashed.

Type Two with a Three Wing (1W3)

We will examine Type Three in detail later on. For the time being, here is a brief summary:

Type Three is variously known as the Achiever or the Performer. As the name suggests, these people tend to be ambitious, enthusiastic and adaptable. They are driven and like nothing more than to accomplish goals and receive validation from others.

A Three wing makes the Two more social and good-humored than a One wing tends to do. It is all about the heart and feelings when it comes to this pairing. Relationships are sought and valued. This combination of types often possesses much charisma and others enjoy their company greatly. They are natural and gracious hosts or hostesses and love to throw parties and gather friends together for celebrations. They have great generosity of spirit and love to give of themselves for the betterment of others.

In times of stress, however, the 2W3, who perceives other's feelings so strongly, can be overwhelmed by the needs of others and even their own repressed emotions. Because types Two and Three both belong in the heart-centered triad, they lack the self-awareness that the influence of a head or body (such as One) type would lend to them. This particular marriage of types can lead to over-sensitivity if they are on the receiving end of criticism. Their sense of pride can become over-inflated, which might lead to authoritarian behaviour and outbursts of anger.

Advice for the Helper

1. Take care to look after your own self-care. You are so busy empathizing with other people and supporting them in their needs, that you forget your own needs in the process. Your own requirements are just as important as everybody else's. It is important to set and maintain your own personal boundaries and to ensure that you get adequate rest, exercise and proper nutrition. Do not change yourself in order to win approval from another. By being yourself and establishing boundaries, you can give to others more authentically, and you can only be of real service to others if you are balanced, healthy and centered within yourself.

2. Before you help somebody, consider whether or not they actually need or want your help in the first place. Have they asked for your assistance? Make sure that you are not just imposing your ideas of the way things should be upon them and interfering unnecessarily. Furthermore, it is not up to you to demand gratitude or decide the manner in which such gratitude is expressed. Instead, try asking people directly what it is they really need. Just because you can sense the need of another, does not necessarily mean that they would like you to step in and 'solve' all their problems for them. You must be willing to accept a "no, thank you" if that is what's forthcoming. This should not be taken as rejection.

3. In the event of you doing something nice for someone, there is no need whatsoever to remind them of it. This is a temptation you need to resist. It will only make the other party question your motivation for helping them in the first place and will cause them to be uncomfortable. They might also withdraw from you altogether, if you choose to behave in this way. Let kindness be its own reward!

4. Understand that people express their affection and appreciation in lots of different ways. Just because it is in a manner that is not instantly recognizable to you and not necessarily a way which you would have chosen yourself, does not mean that they do not care. Learn to recognize the different manifestations of love.

5. Make sure you are honest about your own motives and that you are not lying to yourself about why you are helping someone. If you are just doing it in order to receive gratitude, this is not a healthy motive and you might well be setting yourself up for disappointment. You must guard against co-dependency at all times.

Chapter Four – The Achiever (Type 3)

Also known as the Performer

Fifteen Signs You're an Achiever

1. You like to get things done and are more than willing to work hard to achieve your goals.

2. You can find it hard to slow down and you might struggle to find time to relax.

3. Patience is not one of your virtues!

4. Those around you describe you as a "Type A" personality.

5. You tend to store tension in your chest and heart area.

6. You have no problem setting aside your hobbies to chase success in your primary goal.

7. You love a challenge and relish throwing everything you have into meeting that challenge.

8. If at first you don't succeed, you will try, try, try again.

9. Your biggest fear is failure and this can cause you much stress and anxiety.

10. You focus on appearance. You can become overly concerned with your image and how other people perceive you.

11. A question you are often asked is, "How do you achieve so much?"

12. You very much enjoy a sense of completion and accomplishment. There's nothing like ticking boxes off your to-do list!

13. You are highly competitive and this is something that drives you.

14. You are 'self-made' in some way, having got to where you are in life by hard work and determined pursuit of your goals.

15. You have a lot of energy and others might describe you as having a zest for life which they often find attractive.

What do you think? Have many of the above points resonated with you?

The Achiever: An Overview

As the name suggests, the Type Three on the Enneagram is all about success. It is of vital importance to this type that their success is acknowledged. The Achiever requires this validation in order to feel worthy. They are highly focused, hard-working and competitive. These goals are often in the business world but they are not restricted to this sphere by any means. The Three is commonly a 'self-made' success, often skilled in the art of networking. Generally extroverted, the Achiever can sometimes be charismatic. There is a boundless energy and plenty of drive. Their shadow side is their secret fear of failure.

The Achiever, or the Performer, is frequently image-conscious and as such, can be slow to let his or her real self be shown. This can make intimacy difficult. The Three fears others getting too close lest they discover what they are *really* like.

Because of the Type Three's strong requirement for external validation, they sometimes make the error of chasing external success while ignoring their deeper needs and desires. The Achiever needs to guard against falling in to such a trap.

Notable Three's from the worlds of history, politics, sports and the arts include Bill Clinton, Arnold Schwarzenegger, Oprah Winfrey, Madonna, Lady Gaga, Will Smith, Augustus Caesar, Tony Blair, Andy Warhol, Elvis Presley, Barbra Streisand, Richard Gere, Reese Witherspoon, Anne Hathaway, Justin Bieber, Jon Bon Jovi, Paul McCartney, Lance Armstrong, O.J, Simpson, Truman Capote, Muhammad Ali, Emperor Constantine, Prince William, Carl Lewis, Tony Robbins, Deepack Chopra, Michael Jordan, Sting, Brooke Shields, Tiger Woods, Taylor Swift, Tom Cruise, Demi Moore, Courtney Cox and Kevin Spacey.

The Achiever Levels

Healthy

Authenticity

So genuine and appealing, the Three at their best is literally dripping with gentleness and benevolence. They have learned to fully accept themselves and to listen to their own internal guidance systems. These Threes are everything they appear to be as they have come to understand that they have nothing to hide. They are modest when it comes to their innate strengths and achievements and they are typically big-hearted people with a delightfully self-deprecating humour.

Competence

The high self-esteem of a healthy Three assists them in believing in themselves and their own capabilities. This type is self-assured with plenty of energy to get the job done and get it right. There is an intrinsic self-belief and a deep awareness of their own value as human beings. They are competent and confident enough to adapt to all sorts of situations and remain gracious and charming in the process. Many people will be naturally drawn to a healthy Three.

Ambitious

These Threes are ambitious in the very best sense of the word. Never ruthless, just eager to be the best version of themselves and to fulfill their potential. Self-improvement is a driving force for these people. The healthy Achiever has it in him or her to become an outstanding human, possessing a tremendous amount of admirable qualities. Other people tend to admire them greatly and try to emulate them. This makes the healthy Three a master motivator.

Neutral

Driven

The average Type Three sets great store in doing their job well. Unfortunately, at this level, their motivation for this can be slightly less healthy and based more frequently on an abject terror of failure. They worry very much about what other people think of them and base their self-worth on the achievement of goals. It is said that comparison is the thief of joy. It certainly is for this type. This less than healthy Three will compare his or herself with others in a quest for their own status and self-worth. This is the level of the social climber or the one who believes that a career is everything.

Image-Consciousness

The Achiever can care far too much about how he or she is perceived by others. This can cause them to be "phony" in some ways as they try to conform with the real or imagined expectations of others. They can certainly excel in practicality and efficiency but they risk losing touch with their feelings in their desire to impress. This can lead to issues with intimacy.

Self-Promotion

The intense desire to impress others can cause the Three, at this level of maturity, to promote themselves ceaselessly and aggressively. They might elevate their achievements to this cause. It might feel a little like the childish tendency to say "look at me!" Inflated notions of themselves may arise and they may come across as arrogant and full of contempt, but this is just an attempt to disguise their jealousy.

Unhealthy

Fear of Failure

The Achiever at this level is willing to do or say whatever they consider necessary to preserve their image. Fear of failure and humiliation is intense at this point and can lead them to exploitative and opportunistic behaviours. They will be extremely jealous of another person's success and will strive to preserve their fragile illusion of superiority at all costs.

Deception

These folks can become so terrified at the thought of their mistakes and misdeeds being exposed that they will resort to all sorts of devious behaviours to cover up such failings. This means, of course, that the Achiever at this unhealthy level can absolutely not be trusted. They might betray or sabotage somebody just to get one up on them and their jealous states can border on delusional.

Narcissism

This is the Three at their absolute worst, when their actions correspond with the description of the Narcissistic Personality Disorder. They will stop at nothing to ruin another person's happiness and their destructiveness can become obsessive. The vindictiveness of the profoundly unhealthy Three can border on the psychopathic.

The Achiever Wings

Type Three with a Two Wing (3W2)

When you envisage the "typical" salesperson, you might well be picturing the Type Three with a Two wing. The Achiever's desire to be admired overtakes the Type Two's desire to please others and make them feel good. Although, if it's possible, they may well do both. This variety of the number Three is usually extroverted and can come across as attractive and even seductive. Their persona is cheerful and calm and they will be keen to show their best side and want to be perceived as having it together emotionally.

The influence of the Two wing on the Three personality, can make their "shine" more genuine. At best, this variety of the Three is big on self-observation and likely to be a humble type. They'll also be friendly and likeable with great social skills that cause others to enjoy being around them. The Two wing tempers the Three's hunger to always be the winner. Genuine feelings come to the fore and powerful bonds of friendship can and will be formed.

A healthy Type Three with a Two wing can become an excellent motivational speaker, capable of inspiring great confidence and optimism in others. Uplifting and positive - think Tony Robbins or Oprah Winfrey at their best.

However, when unhealthy, a brittle vanity can come into play for the Achiever with a Two wing. They can lose touch with their genuine innermost feelings while instead constructing a false emotional facade. Self-promotion can become pushy and aggressive, resulting in a lose-lose situation for all involved. They might appear nice and quiet on the outside but the internal reality could be quite unpleasant and destructive.

As outer appearance is important, the 3W2 will typically dress well and in accordance with the latest mainstream fashion. This is because they will want to appeal to the largest possible audience. They might be drawn to "glamorous" work - perhaps on stage, TV, radio, or a high profile position in the business world.

Type Three with a Four Wing (3W4)

Although the Achiever with a Four wing would still like to be admired, they would prefer that this be for their uniqueness rather than appealing to the general masses - a select following rather than mass appeal is what they are aiming for.

The Four wing will tend to make the Three more introverted and less comfortable in social situations, although because of the still dominant Type Three personality, they will be able to hide this with their social competence. They will still be able to hold it all together in times of pressure.

A healthy and mature Achiever with a Four wing is compassionate, gentle and competent. This variant is wise and socially responsible and highly effective in accomplishing their goals, all the while remaining intuitive. A suitable job for this type would be as a career counsellor or a business mentor.

At their absolute best, the Type Three with a Four wing is quietly self-assured while possessed of stunning emotional insight. They teach through example, influencing others through compassionate action. They can be found at the top of organizations or behind the scenes, inspiring others to perform their best.

It is an entirely different story when the Achiever with a Four wing is immature and unhealthy. A lack of balance here will make the Three-influenced drive for success compulsive, while at the same time causing the introspection of the Four to get out of hand. Manipulation comes to the fore and the desire to help is no longer coming from a good place. They are not so great socially and may also indulge in self-deception. They might feel a compulsive need to tell other people about their accomplishments. At their worst, they can be destructive to the self and others.

They like to appear both attractive and unique, wanting to be trend-setters rather than slavishly following the latest fashion. The 3W4 variant is typically drawn to quite showy professions, such as music, politics, broadcasting, the stage, the fashion industry and the sales side of business.

Advice for the Achiever

1. Take a break every now and then from the relentless pursuit of your goals! Your health will benefit and so will your levels of happiness. And let's not forget your loved ones, who will all be pleased to have more time with you. Your goals will still be waiting for you when you wake up from a good night's sleep or return from a holiday. And you will feel refreshed and more effective than ever. Not to mention, nicer to be around. Ambition and determination can be sterling qualities, but they must be tempered by periods of rest which, additionally, allow time for you to reconnect deeply with your inner needs and feelings.

2. Try to be completely honest with yourself. Threes can sometimes get so caught up in trying to play to the peanut gallery that they lose touch with what they really need to be happy. Take time to consider what success actually means to you. What are your values? What makes you happy? Only when you truly connect with the reality of who you are, can you achieve real freedom.

3. As intimacy can sometimes be a challenge for you, it is worth taking the time and trouble to connect with a few chosen people on a deeper level. This takes self-awareness and the willingness to relax and practice appreciation for those you love.

4. It will benefit you greatly to become involved in projects that are unrelated to your ultimate ambition or career goals. It will take you outside of yourself in a healthy way and transcend your preoccupation with the opinions of others.

Chapter Five - The Individualist (Type 4)

Also known as The Romantic

Fifteen Signs You're An Individualist

1. You need a lot of time alone to recharge.

2. You may be an artist – not just a visual artist but perhaps also a dancer, a writer or a musician.

3. You have a tendency to feel melancholy and may get depressed when times get rough.

4. You sometimes feel haunted by the thought that something is missing from your life and this contributes to a deep sense of longing.

5. Authenticity is all important to you, both in your work and in your relationships.

6. You view yourself as being fundamentally different to other people.

7. You are likely to be brutally honest and do not tend to hide your true feelings or motivations from yourself or from others.

8. You are willing to reveal things about yourself that most would never reveal for fear of being embarrassed or ashamed.

9. You have a deep yearning to connect with other people and you tend to feel misunderstood.

10. You've had more than one person in your life tell you that you're 'complicated' or 'weird.'

11. You suffer from low self-esteem and sometimes feel very alone in the world.

12. You are a highly sensitive person, and you have a hard time letting go of past hurts.

13. You'd rather have one close friendship than a hundred superficial ones.

14. Others sometimes accuse you of being moody.

15. Artist or not, you love to surround yourself with art and beautiful things.

Are lots of alarm bells going off in your head right now?

The Individualist Overview

Type Four on the Enneagram likes to think of him or herself as different or unique, indeed basing their very identity on such uniqueness. Feeling different is a double-edged sword to this type. On the one hand, it can cause them to feel special and superior and on the other, isolated and alone.

Enneagram

The Individualist will often be drawn to the arts. They might make a career in this area, becoming dancers, writers, visual artists, musicians or sculptors, for instance. Or maybe they will work closely with artists, perhaps managing museums or galleries or bringing arts to education. Or perhaps they will express this aspect of themselves in the way that they dress or present themselves, or simply in the idiosyncratic lifestyles that they lead.

The sensitivity of this type is heightened and they are emotionally complex souls. Authenticity is all important to the Achiever and he or she longs to be appreciated for his or her own authentic self. This type has no capacity for or interest in shallow relationships. They often feel unappreciated or misunderstood by others and, in these circumstances, will tend to withdraw from the world.

The inner life of the Four is rich and they will spend a lot of time immersed in their own internal world. This activity is important to them and will help them to process their inner feelings. Sometimes, they can express their inner lives in artistic ways. But it is important that they guard against withdrawing from real life completely.

Fours can be haunted by the notion that something fundamental is missing from their lives and this leaves them with a sense of longing, which can morph into melancholy. In times of great stress, this can develop into full blown depression. Self-absorption to an unhealthy level is a trap they can fall into.

It is important for the Individualist/Romantic to strive to be their own savior instead of looking to others to rescue them. They must learn to stand on their own two feet. Be your own rescue, number Four!

Examples of luminaries throughout history who have been Type Fours include: Rumi, Tchaikovsky, Anne Frank, Frida Kahlo, Rudolf Nureyov, Joni Mitchell, Leonard Cohen, Jackie Kennedy Onassis, Chopin, Gustav Mahler, Edgar Allen Poe, Virginia Wolfe, Anais Nin, Anne Rice, Martha Graham, Hank Williams, J.D. Salinger, Tennessee

Williams, Billie Holiday, Cher, Alanis Morrisetter, Florence Welch, from Florence and The Machine, Stevie Nicks, Judy Garland, Cat Stevens, Annie Lennox, Amy WInehouse, Johnny Depp, Nicholas Cage, Angelina Jolie, Marlon Brando, Jeremy Irons, Prince, Kate Winslet and Winona Ryder.

The Individualist Levels

Healthy

Creativity

At his or her best, the healthy Individualist is a profoundly creative being. This creative stream flows strongly and freely, as they express their own personal feelings while at the same time inspiring others to connect with their own creativity and maybe even bring it to new levels. The healthy Four understands that what is personal is universal. She can transform any pain she might have experienced into gold, inspiring others in the process. This constant flow of creativity will enable the Individualist to self-renew and self-generate.

Self-Awareness

The Four's innate tendency for self-reflection leads to a deep understanding of the self that they can also use for the service of others, helping them to understand their feelings and motivations also. They are intuitive, in touch with their inner impulses and sensitive to the extreme, but in a positive way. They help and deal with other people in a compassionate, tactful and gentle way.

Individualism

The clue is in the name! Here, the Four's strong sense of individualism is expressed in a healthy way. The Four at this stage of their development knows him or herself extremely well and is always true to this self. The Type Four at this level is emotionally honest to a fault and has no problem revealing his or her true self, due to the knowledge that the whole range of emotions is common to all. They understand that the courage to show and express vulnerability is actually a strength. Deeply humane, these people can be surprisingly funny, possessing a very ironic view of life. Those around them come to rely on their emotional strength.

Neutral

Romanticism

The Four at this level of maturity strives to create an aesthetically beautiful life for him or herself. This is because a gorgeous environment uplifts them and elevates their mood. This could manifest in a beautiful home with original artwork adorning the walls. Although the Four is not completely immune to image-consciousness, he or she is most concerned with choosing visual art that speaks to his or her soul. The Individualist or the Romantic at this level has a rich fantasy life and places a high value on passion and the imagination.

Self-Absorption

At a somewhat lower level, the tendency of Fours is to disappear too deeply into their own heads. They will internalize everything, becoming unhealthily introverted and overly moody. Here, the Individualist will be self-conscious and shy and will withdraw instead of dealing with their issues and bravely facing the world. They are hypersensitive and will go to great lengths to protect their self-image - essentially staying away from other people, whom they fear might too easily damage it.

Self-Pity

This tendency to go deeply within can descend into the Four living in a kind of fantasy world where they develop a sense of disdain for themselves and others. They can use this as an excuse to be self-indulgent in their emotions and habits and consequently go on to lead decadent and overly sensual lives. A healthy inclination towards daydreaming gets out of hand and they become increasingly unproductive and impractical. The Four might be envious of others at this level of maturity and this makes them even more melancholy.

Unhealthy

Alienation

Unhealthy fours experience alienation from both the self and others. Maybe they have been disappointed by dreams that have not come to fruition or people who have let them down. They will be very angry with themselves and this anger can turn inward and become depression. They feel blocked, both emotionally and creatively and this can expand into a feeling of paralysis. The sense of shame can be deep and all these negative emotions can leave the Four so exhausted that they can barely function.

Self-Contempt

The deeply unhealthy Four treats his or herself with contempt and believes absolutely that this is how other people view them too. They are tormented by desperate thoughts about their failings which sadly lead to feelings of self-hatred. The propensity to blame other people for all this pain results in the Four rejecting anyone who tries to help them.

Despair

A sense of hopelessness abounds and leads to self-destructive thoughts and behavior such as alcohol and drug abuse. Escaping profound pain is the aim here. At its absolute worst, the plight of the unhealthy Four is psychological breakdown or even suicide.

The Individualist Wings

Type Four with a Three Wing (4W3)

Think creativity, curiosity and a lively intelligence. This variant of the Type Three personality has a multitude of ideas and knows how to use them. The rich fantasy life of the Four is married with the drive and capacity for action of the Three, resulting in dreams becoming reality and creative businesses that thrive.

The practicality of the Three balances out the Four's proclivity for drama and melancholy. The focus is very much on career and ambitious goals. The Three wing can give the Four more confidence and extroversion. It can draw the normally introverted Four into more social settings and they might actually be able to enjoy group activities! The Three also lends energy which leads the Fours out of their heads and into the world.

The flip side of this, when the negative aspects of the Four combine with the negative aspects of the Three, is a different story. Then this variant will struggle with shame. They will become obsessive about the image they are projecting and their relationships will be filled with every kind of drama. They may look for a sense of authenticity outside of themselves - where it never is. They will try all sorts of tactics to seek approval, growing angry and competitive in the process. They might even get into financial difficulties as they spend excessively in an effort to impress.

Type Four With a Five Wing (4W5)

The healthy strain of this fusion results in a wonderful blend of the heart and the mind. The Four's inclination to delve deeply into feelings is tempered by the Five's impartiality. This can allow the Individualist to view his or her life in a more objective way - facts are more likely to be brought into play. In addition, the Four's depth of feeling merged with the Five's brain energy creates someone who is both wise and empathetic.

The intellectual capacity of the Five wonderfully complements the profound insight of the Individualist. The Four with a Five wing is a deep, sensitive and perceptive in often ground-breaking ways. They are often quiet and introverted on the outside but there is a lot of activity going on within - both intellectually and emotionally.

When the mix doesn't go so well, the Four with a Five wing can become overwhelmed by out-of-control thoughts and emotions. Their inner life becomes so intense that it is almost unbearable for them. When sufficiently tortured, the 4W5 will withdraw from the world, including from those close to them, feeling painfully alone. Their relationships could suffer and so could their careers. Their inner world becomes their reality and they will reject all offers of help, because they find it hard to trust. They feel that the weight of the world is on their shoulders and can find it a challenge to even look after their own basic needs.

Advice for The individualist

1. Order and discipline are not your natural enemies, especially when they are self-imposed. As a Type Four, you need a healthy dose of discipline to bring your inspired ideas out into the world, for instance, as artistic products or heart-centered businesses. Daydreaming will only get you so far. The world needs dreamers who make their dreams a reality!

2. Guard against your tendency towards self-indulgence, for example, when it comes to food, alcohol or drugs. You can help yourself by striving to maintain balance in your life, fostering healthy habits such as regular sleep, exercise and good nutrition.

3. Do not be a slave to your negative thought patterns. It is all too easy for Fours under stress to fall victim to the demons in their own heads. Find ways to distract yourself when you find yourself heading down a negative path - a favourite comedy show, uplifting music or a walk in the beauty of nature are just some examples. Just don't let yourself go down this route. It is the equivalent of beating yourself up.

4. You are not your feelings. Feelings are of the moment. They are not fixed and they do not define your character - they are not who you are. There is no need to let them lead you astray as they can be very misleading.

5. Don't wait until you are ready to try something or do something. You might never feel ready - a Four seldom will! The trick is to do it scared. To plough on regardless, even if all the pieces do not yet appear to be in place. There is real power in making a start and you will be amazed at how things come together as you go. Just do it!

Chapter Six - The Investigator (Type 5)

Also known as the Observer or the Sage

Fifteen Signs You're An Investigator

1. You have an insatiable need to find out why things are the way they are - scientifically and otherwise.

2. You have a strong urge to question the status quo.

3. You feel that a day in which you haven't learned anything new is a day wasted.

4. If a subject or activity captures your interest, you focus your attention on it intently, until you have fully mastered it.

5. You might have been described by others - either to your face or otherwise! - as eccentric.

6. You hate being pressured into making quick decisions.

7. You are inclined to hold tension in your gut.

8. You might sometimes feel that you are "stuck" in your head and that it takes quite an effort to get back into your body.

9. You are not big on small talk. You find it uncomfortable and, quite frankly, a complete waste of time.

10. Your privacy is of the utmost importance to you and it is quite common for you to experience other people as intrusive.

11. You might feel the need to acquire knowledge and expertise in a bid to overcome deep-seated feelings of inadequacy and self-doubt.

12. You are highly likely to be an expert in your field and that field might be scholarly or highly technical.

13. You have a propensity to withdraw into the safety of your mind when life seems too threatening or overly demanding.

14. You are most probably well-read, not to mention thoughtful and intelligent.

15. It takes you a while to become comfortable with another person, but once you have achieved that level of comfort, you are a devoted companion and that friendship is likely to last a lifetime.

Do you think you might possibly be a Five?

The Inspector Overview

The Investigator spends a lot of time in his or her own head. This is a similarity they have with the Four, but while the Four's comfort zone is in the realm of the imagination and the emotions, the five exists comfortably in the intellect. The Inspector has the habit of retreating into the world of thought when life gets too much. This is their safe place, where they can prepare to face the outside world once again because they like to be prepared and absolutely hate to be put on the spot. They are afraid, in fact, that they don't have what it takes to fully face life.

The Investigator, as the name implies, is sometimes scientifically oriented, but they may also strive for excellence in the area of the humanities.

The type Five can come across as eccentric. This might have something to do with their refusal to bend their beliefs to conform to the mainstream opinion. Freedom of thought is of paramount importance to the Observer, but they can be shy and struggle when it comes to dealing with and expressing their emotions. For this reason, relationships can be difficult for the type Five. This will make them feel lonely at times. Their independent nature can also add to the challenge of relationships, both in the romantic sense, but also when it comes to accepting help from well-meaning people.

The Investigator can be quite a sensitive soul. This makes them feel vulnerable so they commonly adopt coping mechanisms to shield themselves. This can make them come across as intellectually arrogant or carelessly indifferent. This also doesn't help with relationships! But if you learn how to penetrate these barriers, you've got yourself a friend for life.

Because of their need for privacy and fear of intrusion, Fives usually disguise their very strong feelings. This disguise can be extremely effective. For some Fives, one of their biggest fears is of being overwhelmed, so they attempt to keep their lives as simple as possible, making few demands on others in the hope that they will have few demands made on them in return.

Historical or famous Fives of note include: Albert Einstein, Stephen Hawking, Vincent Van Gogh, Georgia O'Keefe, Emily Dickinson, Bill Gates, Eckhart Tolle, Alfred Hitchcock, The Buddha, Oliver Sacks, Edvard Munch, Friedrich Nietzsche, James Joyce, Jean-Paul

Sartre, Stephen King, Salvador Dali, Agatha Christie, Mark Zuckerberg, Kurt Kobain, Peter Gabriel, Marlene Dietrich, Jodie Foster, Gary Larson, David Lynch, Tim Burton, Stanely Kubrick, Annie Liebovitz and Susan Sontag.

The Investigator Levels

Healthy

Visionary

The healthy Five is open-minded to the core. He or she can see the big picture while at the same time, appreciating and comprehending the minutiae. Their view of the world is visionary, seeing everything that can be improved for future generations and having some idea of how to make these improvements happen. They are the pioneers of the world; they are the scientists that make ground-breaking discoveries and the intellectuals that change the way we perceive the forces around us.

Observant

The healthy Five doesn't miss a thing. Their mental alertness is extraordinarily acute and their ability to focus and concentrate is second to none. They are perceptive and insightful with limitless curiosity. Their intellect is always seeking something new to sink its teeth into.

Expert

You will often find a five at the zenith of their chosen filed, as they have a seemingly unlimited capacity to attain mastery of whatever it is that interests them. They find knowledge wildly exciting and their passion often causes them to innovate and invent. Their work is often highly original and of great value to the world. The Investigator at this healthy level is frequently independent and possesses some marvellous idiosyncrasies.

Neutral

Conceptualizing

The Five will usually work everything out in their minds before acting on an idea. This allows them to fine tune everything from the outset. They love to be prepared and have all the required resources at their fingertips. They are studious and hard-working and often become specialists within their fields, while not being afraid to challenge the accepted way of doing things.

Detached

The Investigator, or the Observer, can sometimes become so involved in their intellectual world or the complex project on which they are working, that they become quite detached from reality. They lose touch with the real world, often in quite a disembodied way and become so preoccupied by their visions that matters such as relationships go by the wayside. At this point, the Five displays a kind of high-strung intensity and might even develop a fascination with offbeat or disturbing subjects.

Antagonistic

Beware of trying to interfere with the not-so-mature Five's interior world. They will not thank you for it! They will defend their personal vision at all costs, becoming aggressive and rude with those who oppose their - often radical - views.

Unhealthy

Reclusive

The shyness of an unhealthy Five can go into overdrive. Not only do they become isolated from other humans, but also from reality. Their eccentricity is no longer pleasant and their personality becomes increasingly unstable. They shun company and tend to live a hermit-like existence.

Obsessive

This is obsession in its most unhealthy form. Their ideas become threatening - even to themselves. The Investigator in this state is delusional and suffers from phobias.

Deranged

At the lowest possible level, we are in the area of schizotypal personality disorders. It is a dangerously self-destructive state and psychosis or suicide may be the end result.

The Investigator Wings

Type Five with a Four wing (5W4)

The influence of the Four wing on the Type Five personality can cause them to be more comfortable when it comes to expressing their emotions. They are still curious, reserved and perhaps a little more creative.

It should come as no surprise that the Type Five with a Four wing likes to be alone as both types in their purity enjoy alone time.

The strengths of the 5W4 include a capacity for deep attentiveness and the ability to observe and understand the most tiny details. They think and express themselves creatively and work well independently. But like everyone else, The Type Five with a Four wing is by no means perfect. He or she can be hyper-sensitive and also struggle, at times, to think in a practical and realistic way. They can be too self-absorbed and are prone to distancing themselves from other people.

If you need to communicate with an Investigator with a Five wing, you will do well to be as clear as possible and give them adequate time to process before pressing them for a response. If you are working with them, you would be advised to keep meetings to a minimum, be concise in your explanations and sensitive when giving feedback.

This variant of the Observer is energized by gaining knowledge, new skills and by being appreciated. They will feel drained if they have to spend too much time with other people or forced into situations that overwhelm them. And they certainly do not appreciate harsh criticism!

Type Five with a Six wing (5W6)

When the Six wing is dominant in the Type Five, the Investigator becomes more cooperative. Such a person will also be more inclined to use their impressive knowledge to solve problems rather than to intellectualize. This modification on the Five is inclined to be logical, independent and practical. They desire to be of use and to put their knowledge to work. They want to make the world a better place and feel more worthy in the process.

Their more positive traits include such qualities as focus and good organization, not to mention a passion for learning and improving. They often have a great capacity for solving complex problems and they are the type you want to have around in a crisis as they are adept at remaining calm.

However, the Type Five with a Six wing does have various blind spots. They can have difficulty relating to others and can be overly defensive in their wish to protect their privacy. They can come across as cold and aloof and need to be inspired in order to take any action.

This alternative Investigator loves to solve problems, especially when it makes them feel as if they are making a valuable contribution to society. Their pursuit of knowledge is enthusiastic, particularly when it comes to areas in which they are personally interested. They are drained by spending too much time around others and energized by spending time alone. Always be aware of their propensity for self-doubt in your dealings with them.

Advice for The Investigator

1. Stay in your body. Your intellect is a wonderful tool but it is also necessary to stay connected to other people and to the real world. An excellent way of doing this is by staying in touch with your body and your physical sensations through exercise.

2. Trust is an issue for a Five and because of this, they can find it very hard to open up to other people. When they experience conflict in a relationship, their natural tendency is to withdraw and isolate themselves. This is, of course, not particularly healthy behavior. The Investigator would do well to remember that conflicts are a normal

part of every relationship and the appropriate course of action is to work things out.

3. It is tough for Type Five on The Enneagram to relax. This is because of their innate intensity. It is therefore important for the Five to devise ways to wind down that are suitable and appropriate. Meditation, yoga and running are all recommended.

4. The Five can lose his or her sense of perspective and quite easily feel overwhelmed as there are so many factors to consider! To help you make an accurate assessment in these circumstances, seek out the advice of someone you trust (after first working on your trust issues)!

5. Be selective in the projects you choose to become involved with. Make sure that they are life-affirming and take you in the direction in which you want to go. Make sure you are not distracting yourself in an unworthy way and wasting your precious time.

Chapter Seven - The Loyalist (Type 6)

Also known as the Loyal Skeptic or the Traditionalist

Fifteen Signs You're A Loyalist

1. You hang on to toxic friendships and situations longer than you should.

2. You are perceived - and quite rightly so - as a good trouble-shooter. This is because you are excellent at anticipating problems and devising appropriate solutions.

3. You can hold a lot of tension in the area around your diaphragm.

4. You worry a lot. Let's face it, there are so many things that can go wrong!

5. You are loyal to ideas and belief systems as well as to your friends and family members.

6. You can have trouble connecting with your own inner guidance system. This can cause you to lack confidence in your own judgment.

7. A sense of security is of the utmost importance to you and finding and holding on to this security is a driving force.

8. You tend to ask for advice from many different people before making a decision. As you mature, however, the amount of people upon whose opinion you rely may lessen.

9. You are contradictory in nature and your personality contains many opposites. This is because you tend to go back and forth between various different influences. To paraphrase Walt Whitman - you are large, you contain multitudes!

10. The people around you know that you are reliable and that they can depend on you. You are always there for them.

11. You appreciate order. It is important for you to have a firm structure in place, to have double-checked all your facts and to have a back-up plan.

12. Peace of mind can be elusive for you.

13. You can be suspicious of other people and authorities. You wait until the person or organization has proven themselves fully before giving them your trust.

14. You might have a tendency to act defiantly against whatever it is that you find threatening. In this instance, you may become a rebel and challenge authority.

15. You are responsible, hard-working and trustworthy. Those who are lucky enough to have your friendship know that you will always have their backs.

Did you say "that could be me" more than a few times? If so, read on. You could be a Loyalist!

The Loyalist Overview

As a typical Six, you crave security above all else. This is because you wrestle with a deep-rooted sense of anxiety which is at the core of your being, whether you are aware of it or not.

Type Six on The Enneagram tends to worry a lot. They have no problem imagining all sorts of scenarios, far-fetched or otherwise, in which everything goes wrong. They fear that there is nothing steady enough to hold on to, so they attempt to create such steadiness for themselves, often in personal relationships.

Their propensity to imagine every single possible disastrous outcome makes the Type Six an excellent trouble-shooter, and therefore very useful for others to have around. But this is not much of a comfort for the Loyalist, who struggles to find peace of mind with this constant focus on potential problems.

This can also have the effect of causing the Six to lack spontaneity. Because how can they possibly carry out an action without meticulous planning first? If they don't do this, won't everything collapse like a house of cards?

This is a lot of anxiety to live with. It also makes the Six more suspicious than the average person. You really have to prove yourself to win the Loyalist's trust. But once you succeed in doing so, you have a steadfast friend for life. Loyalty is a fantastic trait, but the Six would do well to make sure they are not staying loyal to someone or something long after it is time to move on from them.

The Six often has a complicated relationship with authority. On the one hand, their desire to have someone or something to believe in might cause them to give their control over to an external force. On the other hand, they also have the propensity to distrust and be suspicious of authority. How confusing! Sometimes a Six individual will lean further in one direction than the other. Sometimes, they might go back and forth between these two different attitudes.

The Loyalist also has two different strategies when it comes to coping with fear. One strategy is phobic, which will cause them to be compliant and cooperative. The other is counter-phobic, which means that the Six will take a defiant stand against anything they find threatening. Rebelliousness and aggression can be the hallmark here.

There have been countless noteworthy Loyalists. Here are a number of them: Sigmund Freud, Robert F. Kennedy, Malcolm X, Diana, Princess of Wales, U2's Bono, Julia Roberts, Ellen Degeneres, Spike Lee, Krishnamurti, Edgar Hoover, George H.W. Bush, J.R.R. Tolkein, Melissa Etheridge, Bruce Springsteen, Mike Tyson, Woody Allen, Sally Field, David Letterman, Newt Gingrich, Jay Leno, Katie Holmes, Benn Affleck, Tom Hanks, Mel Gibson, Diane Keaton, Mark Wahlberg, Dustin Hoffman, Oliver Stone, Michael Moore, John Grisham, Prince Harry, Robert F. Kennedy, Mark Twain and Richard Nixon.

The Loyalist Levels

Healthy

Trusting

This trust is for the self yet it also extends to others. The healthy Six has got the balance right, maintaining their independence while at the same time achieving a cooperative interdependence with others. They are able to collaborate with others and work together in harmony. When the Six learns to believe in herself, she can act with courage and positivity, making her a fabulous leader. She will also be richly self-expressive.

Appealing to Others

When the Six is fully mature and gets her or himself together, they can be a most endearing and lovable type. People react strongly to them in a very positive way and have a genuine affection for them, which they are likely to receive back in kind. Once they have their trust issues sorted out, the healthy Six successfully blends with others, leading to fruitful friendships and alliances.

Dedicated

When the healthy Loyalist finds a movement or an individual in which they fully believe, there is no one who is more dedicated. They will build communities, sacrifice for others or for a greater cause, and bring cooperation, security and stability wherever they go. They are determined, reliable, trustworthy and responsible.

Neutral

Safe

At this neutral level, a kind of contraction occurs and the Loyalist has more of a tendency to play it safe. This is not always a terrible thing. At this point of their development, the Six invests their energy in whatever seems likely to remain stable and secure. They organize and create structure and look to authorities that can promise a sense of continuity. They never let up in anticipating what can go wrong and trying to put systems in place to prevent such problems occurring.

Indecisive

If the Six in neutral mode feels confused or that too many demands are being made on him or her, they will give off many contradictory signals. They will procrastinate and become overly cautious, indecisive and evasive. They will be increasingly negative as their anxiety levels rise and unpredictability results. They may even react in passive-aggressive ways.

Reactive

The fear takes over the Six, although they may not consciously be aware of this. Instead, they blame other people for their uncomfortable feelings, taking it out on the "outsider," for instance. They will be defensive at this level and highly sensitive to threats, constantly monitoring others to work out whether they are a friend or foe. They can be authoritarian and suspicious of everyone and their manner can become belligerent.

Unhealthy

Panicked

Fear takes over at this unhealthy stage. This highly insecure feeling causes the Six to panic and become extremely volatile. They look for increasingly strong authority figures and institutions in order to buoy up their own acute feelings of inferiority and defenselessness. They will be extremely critical and difficult to be around.

Persecuted

This all-pervasive feeling that others are out to get them can make the unhealthy Six lash out irrationally which, in the worst case scenario, can lead to violence.

Hysterical

This is the lowest a Six can go. It is a self-destructive level where alcohol and drugs might be abused. It is the realm of the Paranoid Personality Disorders and they might even attempt to take their own lives.

The Loyalist Wings

Type Six with a Five wing (6W5)

For the most part, the Type Six with a Five wing is a traditional sort, conservative in their views and desirous of fitting into a trustworthy group. Safety is the name of the game here. Although the Six desire to feel secure is colored by the Five need to analyze things right down to their component parts.

When well-balanced, the 6W5 is able to let go of anxiety. This makes them good-humored, relaxed and endearing. They finally feel that they can trust life and in turn, this is a person that can be trusted and relied upon one-hundred-percent.

It is lovely to have the balanced Type Six with a Five wing as a family member. Possessing a quiet confidence, they will be a wonderful companion and source of wisdom. You will be able to develop a deep bond with this type and the Five wing will add a perceptiveness to their enduring friendship.

But imbalance can sometimes ensue and anxiety can rear its ugly head again. They look for a reason for this rising tension and if one is not easily forthcoming, they will find someone to blame for it!

If stress levels increase, the world becomes an increasingly threatening place for the 6W5 and paranoia can begin to set in. They might feel that everybody is out to get them and in this desperately uncomfortable place of tension, they might look for somebody to come to their rescue.

Sixes want to be likable and attractive to others, but Five does not really know how to achieve this. Their attire tends not to be overly showy or flashy.

It may suit the Loyalist with a Five wing to find employment that combines being part of a group with being alone. A forest ranger or a bus driver might be an example of this. Some become involved in risky protection activities such as fire-fighting and others might look for ways to advocate for under privileged people.

The Type Six with a Seven wing (6W7)

The Type Six with a Seven wing is a lot less subdued than the Type Six with a Five wing. Their reactions are more impulsive and colourful and they are less likely to analyze a situation, instead jumping in with both feet. However, the caution of the Six will usually pull back the flamboyance of the Seven before it gets too out-of-hand.

There is a back and forth here between flamboyance and caution which can cause some emotional volatility.

At its best, the Loyalist with a Seven wing is steady, calm and deliberate. When in balance, both the Six's anxiety and the Seven's impulsiveness tend to diminish. They still love having fun with their friends but the desperate drive for security is transformed into an inner strength. They make great parents or siblings.

The 6W7 frequently develops a strong spiritual side, experiencing a deep sense of belonging with the universe. Their faith is a great source of comfort to them.

Of course, things can get out of kilter. If the Type Six with a Seven wing gets out of whack, anxiety and insecurity come to the fore once more. Here, they will jump from one extreme emotional state to the other, desperately searching for someone to help them and feeling increasing despair.

In a more stressed state, the 6W7 can come across as clingy and desperate and this drives other people away. They get themselves into all sorts of trouble as they feel increasingly dependent and tense.

This variant of the Six is often physically attractive and appealing to the opposite sex. In terms of the world of work, they may look to fun professions which also have an element of security inherent in them such as cartoonists or movie reviewers.

Advice for The Loyalist

1. Trust is an issue for you. If you are honest with yourself, you can most probably identify a few people in your life that you can trust completely. Cherish these people and hold them dear. Let them know how much you appreciate them, even though this might make you feel vulnerable. If you genuinely do not have anyone in your life that you feel you can trust, make it a point to find someone, believing that there are trustworthy people out there. You may have to move past your fears to do so, but the end result will be worth it.

2. The Type Six can sometimes use projection as a defense mechanism, in other words, attributing to others what you cannot accept in yourself. This hardly seems fair, does it? Watch out for your tendency to resort to this behaviour. Do not blame others for things that you yourself have done or brought upon yourself in some way. You become your own worst enemy when you become negative and self-doubting, causing even more harm to yourself than you do to others.

3. Do all you can to quell your anxiety. A key step might be to just accept that this is part of your nature and also to acknowledge that more people suffer from anxiety than you probably realize. Try to relax. Everything is going to be fine!

4. Other people like you more than you think they do. That's something else to stop worrying about!

5. Try not to overreact when you are under stress. This involves managing your own thoughts more effectively and acknowledging that most of what you have wasted your time worrying about has never arisen. Fearful thoughts have no purpose but to weaken your ability to act and make things better.

Chapter Eight - The Enthusiast (Type 7)

Also known as the Epicure

Fifteen Signs You're an Enthusiast

1. You are very curious and always looking for new experiences to prevent boredom from creeping in!

2. You are wonderfully optimistic and enthusiastic, something other people often find "catching" and love to be around.

3. You don't store as much tension in your body as other types and tend to be loose and flexible. The challenge for you is to stay grounded.

4. You are not really concerned with the image you project and are more interested in having fun and doing your own thing.

5. Other people accuse you of being restless and may comment that you have trouble settling down to one thing.

6. You see life as an exciting adventure, with something better always around the corner.

7. You are probably an extrovert and great at networking.

8. You don't believe in denying yourself anything - you want to experience all the pleasures that life has to offer.

9. You seek distraction from internal negativity in the external world, for example, by keeping really busy and making sure you are stimulated at all times.

10. You have above average or high self-esteem, believing in your strengths and your talents.

11. You are versatile and can often be multi-talented. Highly practical, you can be engaged in many projects at once.

12. You are most probably intelligent with an agile mind, but not necessarily studious or intellectual.

13. You may have brilliant mind-body co-ordination and manual dexterity.

14. You are naturally good-humored and cheerful, and normally do not take yourself too seriously.

15. You have an over-arching desire to live life to the fullest!

Did you recognize yourself in the above signs? Were you proud? Read on and find out if this is your Type.

The Enthusiast Overview

Enneagram

As far as the Enthusiast is concerned, life is meant to be one big, exciting adventure from start to finish. This makes them fun to be around and people are naturally attracted to their *joie de vivre*. They are always looking to the future and looking forward to something better that's around the next corner.

Most Sevens are extroverted. They have tons of energy which they like to expend in all sorts of ways, being multi-talented and creative. Indeed, they are highly practical with multiple skills and may possess an entrepreneurial spirit. If they do have a flaw in this regard, it is that they sometimes have difficulty focusing. Also, they have so many interests and such high hopes for the "next big thing" that they can find it hard to settle on just one project and bring it fully to fruition. They will, however, be adept at promoting themselves and their product, business or service and they are natural networkers.

Sevens do not believe in denying themselves and they can be compulsive pleasure seekers. They sometimes use this activity to distract themselves from anything negative that might be going on in their lives. This may lead to a tendency towards addiction - drugs, gambling, etc.

The typical Enthusiast, or Epicure, as he or she is also known, is usually not lacking in confidence. While this is healthy, this can at times veer towards being self-centered or having an inflated sense of entitlement.

The Seven does not always like confronting the harsh realities of life and other people's problems, but if they run away from confronting such emotions, they run the risk of storing up problems for themselves and suffering from anxiety or depression down the road.

Of course, there have been loads of famous Sevens. Some you have most probably heard of are: The Dalai Lama, Mozart, John F. Kennedy, Richard Branson, Bette Midler, Goldie Hawn, Robin Williams, Galileo Galilei, Thomas Jefferson, Amelia Earhart,

Kandinsky, Noel Coward, Joe Biden, Silvio Berlusconi, Suze Orman, Elton John, Fred Astaire, Joan Rivers, George Clooney, Jim Carrey, Leonardo DiCaprio, Cameron Diaz, Simon Cowell, Larry King, Howard Stern, David Duchovny, Robert Downey Junior, Brad Pitt, Cary Grant, Stephen Spielberg, Russell Brand, Miley Cyrus, Sacha Baron Cohen and Sarah Palin.

The Enthusiast Levels

Healthy

Joyful

The Enthusiast at his highest level is all gratitude and appreciation for everything he has, including all the simple pleasures in life. This ability to assimilate experiences in an in-depth way leads to a kind of ecstasy that borders on the spiritual.

Enthusiastic

Well, it is their name! This extroverted type is good-humored, lively and spontaneous. They respond to everything in an excitable and eager way, finding even "normal" life experiences quite invigorating.

Multi-talented

Their many gifts make them accomplished and productive - well able to achieve in lots of different areas. Due to their enthusiasm for a broad range of subjects, they can often be compelled to develop a variety of skills.

Neutral

Restless

So many choices, so little time - this could be the mantra of the average Enthusiast. They have a fear of missing out which makes it difficult for them to choose between one option and another. Focus can be difficult to achieve as they are constantly seeking out new adventures. They can be sophisticates at this stage in their maturity. They like variety, plenty of cash and keeping up with the latest fashion.

Hyperactive

The fear of being bored keeps the Seven at this level in constant motion. They don't know what they need to feel satisfied so they throw themselves into perpetual activity. They will perform and exaggerate and behave in more and more flamboyant ways. They will find it difficult to follow through on their ideas.

Consuming

They never feel that they have enough. They consume to excess, whether that be shopping, food or drugs. They are never satisfied, no matter what, and this can lead them to be demanding and hardened.

Unhealthy

Addicted

The unhealthy Seven does not know when to stop. They cannot control their impulses and so desperate are they to soothe their anxiety. They can sink to levels of depravity and their behavior may become abusive and offensive.

Out of Control

From bad to worse! In a desperate bid for escapism, these Sevens are incapable of dealing with anxiety properly and may descend into erratic or impulsive actions.

Self-Destructive

The lowest possible level for the Seven to sink to. They have probably ruined their health at this point and given up on themselves and life. They're most likely deeply depressed and may attempt suicide. Their symptoms here would not be dissimilar to bipolar disorder.

The Enthusiast Wings

The Seven with a Six wing (7W6)

The hallmarks of a Seven with a Six wing are that they are enthusiastic and adventurous - as you would expect with a seven - but with a healthy dose of responsibility thrown into the mix. Sounds like quite a good balance, doesn't it? They still love to pursue new experiences but they are much better able to stick to prior commitments.

Although this all sound perfect, there is a potential downside too: a Fear of Missing Out (FOMO)! The Seven with a Six wing really wants to honor their commitments, but what if a wonderful last minute opportunity arises? You can see how this variant of the number Seven is likely to feel torn. They want, most of all, to feel happy and fulfilled and the way the Seven goes about this is by finding joy in even the smallest of experiences. But the Seven with a Six wing might have a tendency to rationalize away negative feelings, unconsciously convincing themselves of their own happiness when this is, in fact, not the case.

They will go to great lengths to avoid being upset - even rationalizing and justifying the bad behavior of others, because they value happiness and optimism above all else. Relationships are very important to them, as is pleasure-seeking on all levels and this all abiding fear of missing out on potential opportunities.

The Enthusiast with a Six wing has many positive traits. The inclination is to be highly productive. They also cooperate well with others, whether they are fellow workers, clients or other collaborators. They manage to remain sensitive to the feelings of others, not riding roughshod over their emotions in the pursuit of their own goals and happiness. Even when confronted with a stressful situation, the Seven's optimism will pull them through and allow them to remain buoyant. They are quick thinkers but do not merely consider the surface issues. They are capable of going deep and considering matters in a thorough way.

But, of course, we all have our blind spots to contend with and this variant of the Type Seven is no exception to that rule. Unlike the "pure" Type Seven, the Seven with a Six wing cares deeply about what other people think of them and is easily affected by their opinions. This might cause them to doubt themselves and lead to a feeling of all-pervading anxiety. And the Seven's propensity to become bored does not go away. They may easily become restless in a job or a relationship and crave something new. And when stress hits, the Enthusiast with a Six wing could struggle with organization and focus.

When dealing with an Enthusiast with this wing, you will do well to remain optimistic and upbeat and to really listen to them, taking all their ideas seriously. They love to chat in a free-flowing, light-hearted way and they also greatly appreciate encouragement and support. This will especially be the case when they are expressing difficult emotions, which they find challenging.

Remember how much they are energized by new ideas and experiences and how creativity inspires them. They love meeting new people and going to places where there are large gatherings of folk to get to know. Take your 7W6 to a party or a concert. They will love you for it!

What they do not thrive on is overly rigid schedules or rules. Do not beat them down with negativity and make sure that the Seven with a Six wing in your life has plenty of company to keep them happy and energized. They absolutely hate routine and thrive on lots of interesting choices - not to mention the freedom to make such choices.

In summary, the Enthusiast with a Six wing is a curious type and can be wildly productive given the right circumstances. Although they still seek new experiences, they are steadfastly loyal to friends and family. Creative and adventurous, they also love to build a sense of community. They are sometimes known as "The Pathfinder."

Type Seven with an Eight wing (7W8)

The Eight wing lends a toughness to the Type Seven. It also inclines them to be more work-oriented. They are still enthusiastic - as the main hallmark of umber Seven on The Enneagram - but they have an added determination.

In a general sense, there is still a fear of missing out, but this manifests itself more in a fear of deprivation rather that a fear of missing out on excitement. The pursuit of new opportunities is still a high priority and so is the dislike of rigidity and scheduling. The Seven's basic desire to be happy and fulfilled is tempered somewhat by the Eight wing and can now be more accurately described as a wanting to be satisfied and content.

Although they still love to be out in the world, going to events where there are lots of people, such as big parties and festivals and also travelling to exotic places, the Eight wing gives a more protectionist dimension to the Seven's actions and they defend themselves by justifying the poor behavior of others and by rationalizing away their own bad feelings.

Optimism is still a top priority for the Seven with an Eight wing, as is personal gratification. They are always on the lookout for new opportunities and consider it highly important to be open to new experiences. Fear of missing out does not go away with the presence of the Eight wing. They still crave and adore the company of other humans and will justify the negative actions of such humans to prevent themselves from feeling bad.

This variant of the Seven wing has many attributes. They have a knack for remaining positive, no matter what, and staying in that all-important high energy mindset. Self-confidence comes to them easily and they often have a natural charisma that attracts other people like bees around a honey pot. They are no shrinking violets either, and are able to stand up for and assert themselves. They are a good sort to have around you in a crisis, as they have the ability to remain calm in situations where many people are in a panic.

Like everyone else, however, the Enthusiast with an Eight wing has weaknesses that they must strive to overcome. The Eight wing does make the all-encompassing charm of the number Seven slightly less pervasive. Because of this, the Seven with an Eight wing can come across as quite blunt at times. They may offend people without realizing or without meaning to do so. They can also be impatient with situations and people. The Enthusiast with an Eight wing might be accused of focusing too much on their career and to the detriment of other aspects of their lives such as their relationships. They might be overly materialistic also, forgetting what is truly important in life. In spite of all this, they could still suffer from the Type Seven tendency to have difficulty following through on plans, once the initial enthusiasm has worn off.

When you are communicating with this alternative to the Type Seven, they will really appreciate it if you listen carefully to them. This is because they love to have conversations and expressing themselves is very important to them. They like their conversations to have a purpose, not just to wander aimlessly and their preference is to keep things upbeat. They want to get right to the point while also having the opportunity to share every single thought and idea that is going on inside their heads. They appreciate people being direct and honest with them and will happily cooperate to reach a compromise if an argument arises.

If you have a Seven with an Eight wing in your life, never lose sight that they love new experiences, especially fun occasions such as parties and celebrations, concerts and festivals and travelling to new and far flung destinations. Relationships are a big priority for them and you will get on better with your 7W6 if you allow them to be the center of attention from time to time! And they dearly love a good goal to accomplish.

Do not cut off their energy with rigid rules and limits. They hate, above all, to feel controlled. They also thrive on company - so why not give them yours?

The Type Seven with an Eight wing is sometimes known as the Opportunist.

Advice for The Enthusiast

1. You love to have conversations and express all your many varied opinions, but be honest with yourself. Are you *really* listening to those with whom you are having conversations?
Active listening is an art worth cultivating. Think of all the new and interesting things you'll discover if you really take in what other people are saying to you. It might even lead to new opportunities. And there doesn't always have to be chatter. Silence is golden. Do not be afraid to put down your phone or turn off the TV. There are real and lasting benefits to be had from not distracting yourself all the time and staying present with your thoughts and emotions. Living with less external stimulation in this way, will help you to trust yourself. You might even be more satisfied when you start doing less. Now doesn't that sound like a huge relief?

2. Life is long and you don't have to experience everything all in one go. Imagine having every dinner you were ever going to eat all in one day! You would not want that. So that tempting car or cake, for instance, will still be in the show room or the shop next week – there may even be a better alternative. Let go of your compulsive fear of missing out on opportunities. They will come around again and you will be better able to judge which ones are really meant for you.

3. As a typical Seven, you would be well advised to observe your impulses instead of diving in head first. Do not give into them straight away, no matter how much you might want to do so. Instead, learn to judge which ones are worthy of acting upon. Not all impulses are created equally! As you become more observant and a better judge of all your different impulses, you will learn which ones are worth your focus, time and energy, and you can start living your life in a more beneficial way.

4. Experience is not all about quantity. It is about quality too. In other words, a few wonderful and deeply felt experiences can be better than a thousand scattered ones where you do not really allow yourself to be present. Good advice for the Seven is to stay in the moment and pay attention to what you are actually doing in the now, instead of constantly anticipating potentially better experiences. The latter is not the path to true satisfaction.

5. Question your desires. Is what you want really what you want? When you consider the likely long-term consequences of your current desires, do you still think you're longing for the right thing for you? Or will it only lead to disappointment or even unhappiness in the long run? Practice discernment at all times.

Chapter Nine - The Challenger (Type 8)

Also known as the Ruler

Fifteen Signs You're a Challenger

1. You like to be in charge. And why on earth *wouldn't* anyone put you in charge of things?

2. You hate, hate, hate to be controlled. In fact, you rarely let this happen to you and anyone who tries is met with a lot of attitude.

3. Others might accuse you of being domineering.

4. You have the capacity to work extremely hard in order to manifest your goals.

5. You are an excellent mentor and can effectively show others how to achieve as you have done, thus nurturing the leaders of the future.

6. You have a propensity for getting bored very quickly. This can also lead to impatience.

7. You can come across as somewhat fierce and others can find you intimidating at times.

8. Anger can be an issue for you and you are inclined to lose your temper fairly easily. Some people find this scary!

Enneagram

9. As the name of this type implies, you love to take on a challenge and indeed, enjoy giving other people challenges too, thereby helping them to stretch their abilities and even to exceed themselves.

10. You have an in-built charisma or magnetism. This makes you an effective leader, no matter what sphere you live and work in. You can quite easily persuade others to follow you.

11. You have great energy and you use this - together with your formidable willpower - to leave your mark on society

12. You value independence highly and you are not afraid to stand alone, defying social convention if necessary.

13. You possess a steely determination which others find amazing and sometimes even logic-defying.

14. You have a powerful 'can do' attitude and tend to be extremely resourceful. You get things done, in a commanding way.

15. You have an abundance of common sense and this can greatly benefit those around you.

So what do you think? Are you a Challenger? Other people can offer their opinions but only you know for sure.

The Challenger Overview

Control is at the heart of the Challenger's personality. At their core, they are totally unwilling to be controlled, whether it be by a person or by circumstances. It is of the utmost importance to an Eight that they remain the masters of their fates and the captains of their souls. The flip side of this is that they are inclined to be domineering. This coupled with their unwillingness to be controlled may lead them to try to control others. Ironic, is it not? A healthy Challenger is well able to keep this tendency under control but it is something that always has to be guarded against, especially as one moves down the maturity scale. It can be a recurring issue in the interpersonal relationships of an Eight.

Eights take the concept of being strong-willed to new heights. They are tough-minded to a fault and their enormous energy and practical nature aids them significantly in getting their own way.

The Challenger desires to get the most out of life and this can often extend to their physical appetites. They indulge in those appetites without experiencing a hint of unhealthy remorse.

Financial independence is a massive priority for the Challenger. He or she may have difficulty having a boss. They do know best, after all! Challengers tend to benefit from working in a field where they can be their own boss. Under certain circumstances, an Eight may feel the need to opt out of society altogether, finding other ways to gain financial freedom instead, as they are usually uncomfortable with hierarchies.

The Challenger has a deep and abiding fear of feeling vulnerable. This can be detrimental to their capacity to form intimate relationships because, obviously, intimacy requires vulnerability. Defenses need to be lowered! Of course, this involves letting go of the need to be in control and trust is of the greatest importance in this arena. Betrayal of any kind will cut the challenger to the quick. Woe betide the person who violates an Eight in this way!

Believe it or not, Eights can be sentimental. They hide it well, even from those closest to them, but it's true. This is an indication of how much the Eight fears being vulnerable. However, if you do manage to win their trust, you will have someone who stands by you no matter what. The Challenger is hugely protective of those in their inner circle - family and friends especially - and they will move mountains to provide for these people.

A big Achilles Heel for the Eight is their anger. At lower levels of maturity, this emotion can spiral out of control and turn into rage. Such aggression can even turn into violence and unhealthy Eights can be intimidating, ruthless and even dangerous.

Not surprisingly, there are many Eights who have achieved remarkable feats of success in this life. Some examples of these include: Winston Churchill, Oskar Schindler, Martin Luther King, Serena Williams, Barbara Walters, Toni Morrison, Frank Sinatra, Bette Davis, Paul Newman, Richard Wagner, Franklin D. Roosevelt, Fidel Castro, Lyndon Johnson, Golda Meir, Saddam Hussein, Donald Trump, Ernest Hemingway, James Brown, Queen Latifah, Aretha Franklin, Pink, Jack Black, Sean Connery, John Wayne, Mae West, Humphrey Bogart, Jack Black, Dr Phil, Roseanne Barr, Jack Nicholson, Tommy Lee Jones, Clint Eastwood, Lauren Bacall, Chrissie Hynde, Courtney Love, Pablo Picasso, Norman Mailer, Senator John McCain and last but not least, Indira Gandhi.

The Challenger Levels

Healthy

Heroism

Enneagram

Not unlike Type One on the Enneagram, Type Eight possesses the qualities that heroes are made of. There is the potential here to climb awesome heights and to achieve historical greatness. At the peak of his or her health and maturity, an Eight can restrain their lesser impulses and become a truly magnanimous individual, attaining true self-mastery. Possessing massive courage, they are willing to face real danger in order to achieve their vision and make a true difference.

Strong

This strength comes with a remarkable self-confidence and self-assertiveness. They have no problem standing up for their needs and wants. The Eight at this healthy stage is full of drive and passion and no one is more resourceful than them. A 'can do' attitude is dominant in these types.

Authoritative

The natural leader or commander. The Eight will be the one who is not afraid to take the initiative to get things done and make things happen. Decision-making comes easily to them as they rarely doubt their own judgment. They are the people's champion. They will provide and protect and carry those who lack their strength. They are truly honourable.

Neutral

Self-sufficient

It is of utmost importance to the Challenger, at this stage of their development, that they have adequate resources, financially and otherwise. To this end, they will become profoundly pragmatic and enterprising. They will be the quintessential 'wheeler-dealer,' willing to deny even their own emotional needs as they take any necessary risks and put their noses to the grindstone.

Domineering

At this not-so-mature level, the Challenger will seek to bend others' wills to their own. They have no compunction about imposing their vision on everyone else. Dominating other people, and equally their environment, the Eight will become a 'show off' and overly forceful. They do not appreciate anybody who has the temerity to question their word or their decisions and they must feel that people are supporting their efforts. They become egocentric at this point and forget to treat other individuals with the respect that they want and deserve.

Intimidating

Matters go from bad to worse - for Eights and those around them - as we travel further down the maturity ladder. This is where the Challenger becomes more than challenging - they become adversarial, belligerent and confrontational. They will refuse to back down, even if they secretly suspect that they are wrong. This would be tantamount to losing face and they cannot allow that to happen! They will threaten and impose punishments in order to extract obedience from those around them, who at this stage are feeling increasingly insecure. They are their own worst enemies however, as their attitude and actions may well backfire, turning people against them and perhaps even causing them to join together against the Eight.

Unhealthy

Ruthless

At this immature level of development, things start to get quite nasty. Here the Eight will stop at nothing to get their own way including immoral behaviour and violence. If they are in a position to get away with being dictatorial, then they certainly will! They might resort to criminal behaviour, not caring if they rip people off. They will defy all attempts to control them.

Delusional

Oh dear! At this stage of bad emotional health, the Eight will think that he or she is invincible. Their antics will now border on megalomania and extreme recklessness will be the order of the day. They believe they are truly invulnerable.

Vengeful

"Never surrender!" will be their battle-cry, but not in a good way. At the lowest of the low, the Challenger will destroy everything and everyone that does not bend to their will. They will descend to all sorts of barbaric conduct, even murder. We are in the territory here of the sociopath.

The Challenger Wings

The Eight with a Seven wing (8W7)

A person doesn't get any tougher than the Type Eight with a Seven wing. They might even look tough, with broad, rough features and an enormous, muscular physique. And their actions might well match their appearance. This is because the Challenger with a Seven wing has so much powerful energy coursing through their system. The Eight's overpowering personality tends to dominate quite a bit and values being in charge above all else, including the Seven's need to be the life and soul of the party.

Their mode of appearance can vary wildly. When they are in the mood and the circumstances are right, they might be very well dressed and 'pulled together.' But at other times, when they are preoccupied, they might not be bothered at all about what they look like.

Of course, every single personality has the capacity to shine and the Eight with a Seven wing is no exception to this. When they're well-balanced, an 8W7 can be charming and tactful. If they have a sense of self-awareness, this can make them less aggressive and less extreme in their conduct. They realize that real power comes from within and that they do not have to put on a show of strength. They discover patience and learn to calm their more destructive impulses.

At their peak, the Challenger with a Seven wing will choose kindness instead of being argumentative. Picture a gentle giant. They will use their power for good, becoming considerate and perceptive in their dealings with people. They get in touch with their intuition and this allows them to accurately judge various situations. The highly integrated 8W7 has options available to him or her which are not possible at a lower level.

But with the good comes the bad. The Challenger with a Seven wing can actually be a physical danger to others. Insensitive, unsociable, with no regard for the rules that govern a civilized society, the 8W7 becomes a very rough character indeed. Think, here, of the quintessential bully or thug.

With even less integration, this variant of the Eight will lash out violently. He or she will be judgmental, defensive and intolerant. Their mantra is 'kill or be killed.'

In terms of professions that suit this type of Eight, they may include things like construction foreman, army general, or boxer. Of course, they can also be a stay-at-home mother! It is all possible.

The Eight with a Nine wing (8W9)

Physical power is still a huge component when it comes to the Challenger with a Nine wing. But Type Nine on The Enneagram has a passive quality causing this particular personality to be quiet but aggressive when provoked. Imagine a bear, normally slow-moving but capable of sudden violence. Eruptions of anger are possible. They usually move around quite slowly but they must feel that the situation is under control before they can relax.

When well-balanced, this variant of the Eight is a joy to be around. They will be kind and gentle and in touch with their inner guidance. They will not feel the need to dominate. Neither will they feel an impulse to withdraw. They wield their power wisely, knowing when it is of benefit to themselves and others to do so, and sensing when it is not.

At the very top level, the 8W9 possesses a powerful benevolence and has the capacity to be a great leader or teacher. They are tough when it is needed and gentle when that is what is required.

But when unhealthy, the Eight with a Nine wing develops a deep conflict within and becomes unpredictable and dangerous to be around. When they are quiet, you can be sure that there is anger lurking just beneath the surface. This can result in frequent explosions of rage.

At their worst, they can descend into a state of paranoid isolation. Intrude and you might be attacked or killed by this antisocial being who lacks compassion or conscience.

The Challenger with a Nine wing will normally not care about what they look like. They would rather just relax. They prefer jobs that mean they will not be overly bothered by other people. A truck driver or a night guard might be a good example. Of course, as with any type, you can find them anywhere!

Advice for The Challenger

1. It is absolutely the case that you value your independence and this is not necessarily a bad thing. However, people need people, whether you like it or not and it is going to be necessary for you to let others in. It is not possible to function in this world as an island and people are not as expendable as you think they are. For example, you might need employees who are loyal and that you can trust. If you alienate them, you will lose them. Similarly, in your personal life, you will be isolated and lonely unless you let people in.

2. Choose your battles wisely! You don't have to win every battle and every argument. Let others have their way from time to time. It is not true power to 'beat' other people all the time. If you feel the need to dominate, it means that your ego is out of control and this will just lead to more unhealthy conflict. Avoid this.

3. Realize your true gifts and capacities, and use your power for good. Restrain yourself if you can foresee that your actions are likely to hurt others. Your real power is to motivate, uplift and to show others what they, too, are capable of. In this way, you can be of great service to others, perhaps helping them in a crisis. This is absolutely the way to inspire loyalty from people.

4. Another quick word about power: those who are attracted to you because of your power and because of this alone, have no real affection for you. They might just be using you as you use them back. Is this really how you want to live your life?

5. People are nicer than you think. So let them in, knowing that this is a sign of true strength and not weakness. When you are mistrustful of others, they will pick up on this and they will not be favorably disposed towards you. Instead, find out who you can trust and show these loyal friends and colleagues your appreciation and devotion.

Chapter Ten - The Peacemaker (Type 9)

Fifteen Signs You're a Peacemaker

1. Your dearest wish is to avoid conflict at all costs. This makes some people perceive you as agreeable and others view you as too passive.

2. You are an expert at seeing all points of view and every side of the argument.

3. You have difficulty establishing firm personal boundaries.

4. You are capable of bringing warring parties together and can be instrumental in healing conflicts.

5. You may have a tendency to suffer from lower back pain.

6. You have an active interest in the spiritual side of life.

7. When in an intimate relationship, you have a propensity to give up your agenda in favor of your partner's. You tend to merge with your nearest and dearest. This might result in you neglecting your own personal needs and desires.

8. You dislike having to confront the unpleasant aspects of life. Sometimes you run away from them or live in denial.

9. You are likely an introverted person.

10. Your friends would describe you as easy going, reliable, tolerant and likable.

11. Your inclination is to see the best in other people and to have a trusting and optimistic view of life.

12. You probably find great joy and solace in the natural world.

13. You can sometimes be uncomfortable with change and this can cause you to be conservative – but you are more adaptable than you give yourself credit for!

14. Because you are so modest, some people might make the mistake of taking you for granted or overlooking the often significant contributions that you make.

15. You may have been brought up in an environment where you were taught that conflict is bad and something that should be avoided or denied.

Did anything sound familiar? More than one thing? Then you just might be a Peacemaker.

The Peacemaker Overview

As the name implies, Type Nine on The Enneagram, the Peacemaker, is a seeker of harmony in all areas of life.

Conflict is the enemy itself, as far as the Nine is concerned, and they will avoid it like the plague, if at all feasible. This can be a challenge because, as we all know, conflict is an integral part of life and practically impossible to avoid. So the Peacemaker has to develop strategies to side step these clashes. These often include some manner of withdrawal. This means that Nine is commonly an introvert. Even if the Peacemaker is particularly social, they will find ways to remove themselves from potential strife that may arise within their circle of friends. Because of this, their habit is to go with the flow. Others view them as tolerant and easy going and consequently, easy to like.

The Peacemaker holds a positive view of life and of those that surround them. They are inclined to give people the benefit of the doubt, assuming that they are good sorts until the opposite is proven. They are trusting - as well as trustworthy - and they see the glass as being half-full rather than half-empty. It is common for them to have a stalwart faith - spiritual or otherwise - that things are always working out for them.

A deep-seated desire for the Nine is a sense of connection. They feel this connection with both their fellow humans and with the natural world. The Peacemaker has a genuine connection to nature and will have a sense of being at home wherever it is green. Another arena where the Nine feels at home is parenthood. This type is often an excellent parent - loving and attentive.

Change can sometimes be a challenge for the Type Nine, causing them to feel uneasy and uncomfortable. They do like to stay in their comfort zones! This can translate into quite a conservative attitude towards life. When a Nine is not so well-developed emotionally, they can suffer from a sort of inertia. This can prevent them from taking the action necessary to bring required change into effect. But when change does

Enneagram

manifest itself, the Peacemaker may well surprise him or herself with how adaptable they are and how they are, in fact, more than capable of adjusting to their new circumstances. They might also find that they are more resilient than they themselves suspected.

Sometimes they do not give themselves enough credit and this can be quite a problem in their lives. Due to this innate humility and refusal to hog the limelight, the Nine might find him or herself being taken for granted by others. It can almost feel to the Peacemaker like people don't even see them. This lack of validation can be hard to take and they may feel invisible. It is a real shame, as the Peacemaker is capable of and frequently does make significant contributions to many situations. This might show itself as a deep sadness that few are aware of. Or it might be an anger that builds up inside and erupts every so often in a short-lived burst of temper. Or, alternatively, it may reveal itself in passive-aggressive behavior.

It is characteristic of the Nine that they do not always have a definite sense of self and of their own identity. They don't really know who they are! This is only heightened by their penchant to almost merge with their loved ones. They virtually take on the characteristics of those closest to them through a process of identification. So if you are a Nine and you are reading this, it is possible that you do not recognize yourself!

There have been many famous Nines dotted throughout history and prominent in our society today. These include: Queen Elizabeth II, Abraham Lincoln, Carl Jung, Walt Disney, Gloria Steinem, Audrey Hepburn, George Lucas, Princess Grace of Monaco, Claude Monet, Dwight D. Eisenhower, Ronald Reagan, Joseph Campbell, Gary Cooper, Carlos Santana, Tony Bennett, Sophia Loren, Whoopie Goldberg, Geena Davis, Lisa Kudrow, Woody Harrelson, Kevin Costner, Audrey Hepburn, Annette Bening, Jimmy Stewart, Janet

Jackson, Ringo Starr, General Colin Powell, John F. Kennedy Jr., Gerald Forde, Norman Rockwell, Jim Henson and John Goodman.

The Peacemaker Levels

Healthy

Self-Possessed

At their peak, Nines are a joy to be around. And it is a joy, in fact, to be one of them! They feel enormously fulfilled by all that life has given them and they are, therefore, supremely content. They feel totally present within themselves. This causes them to have a sense of, not only independence, but an intense aliveness. They are adept at forming profound relationships with others because of this powerful sense of connection.

Serene

This serenity is often derived from a profound feeling of acceptance. This in turn leads to an enormous sense of stability. They do not doubt themselves and neither do they doubt others. Total trust is the order of the day. There is a perception of ease that they bring to everything that they do, largely because they are patient, good-humored and unselfconscious. They are not trying to be anything that they are not and are genuinely lovely people. There is a simple innocence and a lack of pretense which makes the deeply receptive and healthy Nine a pleasure to be around.

Supportive

Enneagram

The support that the Peacemaker lends to others carries with it a healing and calming influence. They are fantastic at bringing people together and harmonizing disparate groups. Their optimism reassures others. All the above, together with their often excellent communication skills, can make the Nine a marvellous mediator.

Neutral

Self-Effacing

This mode of conduct is often designed to avoid conflict as much as possible. They do not want to rock the boat so, consequently, will put up with a lot. They might become accommodating to a fault and go along with other people's wishes. This could make them agree to do things that they really do not want to do. This is not a good scenario for anyone involved!

Another way the Five might seek to avoid rocking the boat is by fitting themselves into conventional roles. They do not relish defying other people's expectations. An example of this is a woman becoming a wife and mother. Then, if she returns to work when her children are older, she might go into a traditionally 'feminine' profession such as nursing or hairdressing. This is not the type that commonly challenges stereotypes.

Disengaged

This tendency is due to their wish to avoid problems and conflict of any sort. They might still be taking part in their normal activities but they will be 'checked out' in some way. You might see it in their eyes! They are purposely not paying proper attention. They will not reflect on what is happening because they simply do not want to! They can become complacent, putting up with situations that are not necessarily ideal but are too much trouble to confront. Because of this, they will deny problems and have an impulse to 'sweep them under the rug.' They construct a comforting fantasy world for themselves which is so much more pleasant than reality. The Peacemaker can develop indifference as a coping mechanism, as they refuse to focus on problems and retreat from the real world into self-imposed oblivion.

Resigned

This resignation is in a bid to have peace at any price. A kind of fatalism creeps into the atmosphere. Why bother trying to change anything when it will not work anyway? They can be very stubborn in this stance, causing those around them to get annoyed and frustrated with them as they struggle to get a meaningful response or make things happen. They may indulge in wishful thinking and imagine all sorts of possible magical solutions. They will appease others in order to avoid trouble, even when this is not the healthiest solution.

Unhealthy

Repression

The propensity to hold everything in becomes increasingly unhealthy. It makes the Nine incapable of facing problems as they disassociate themselves from all conflicts. The self cannot be fully actualized in these circumstances and the Peacemaker remains in an undeveloped state. This can actually constitute a danger to those around them as their conduct here can be neglectful.

Disassociation

At this point, the Peacemaker disassociates from life to such an extent that they can barely function. A sort of numbness sets in, while they block out awareness of anything that might upset them.

Catatonic

At this most extreme of lows, the Nine will come across as really disoriented, seemingly becoming nothing more than a shell of their former selves. Psychological conditions can arise, such as schizoid and dependent personality disorders. Multiple personalities are also possible.

The Peacemaker Wings

Type Nine with a One wing (9W1)

The Type Nine with a One wing is a big softy! The influence of the Nine will remain mostly dominant, which will result in the intellectuality of the One filtering in, but not being subject to a great deal of reality-testing. This can cause the Nine with a One wing to develop a set of beliefs that might come across as a bit weird to others. They may be strongly superstitious and 'airy fairy.' The Peacemaker with a One wing can actually make this work for them!

The 9W1 is refined and possesses a manner of elegant poise. In style of dress, they will strive to be as inconspicuous as possible, choosing clothing that will enable them to fit in and become as invisible as possible. Mainstream fashion is the order of the day, with no flamboyant statements being made! They do have a desire to be perfect, however, because of their One wing, so their attire is likely to be neat and tidy.

They are not the workaholics of the Enneagram and can be partial to a pleasant afternoon nap!

When in a healthy state of mind, the One wing lends the type Nine more presence. The light is on *and* someone is home! Concrete results are more likely when the goal-setting One wing exerts its influence. The Peacemaker will become more ambitious but will not be prey to as much perfectionism as the Type One in their pure state. By their efforts, this variant of the Type Nine can affect others in a positive and useful way. However, this is done in a subtle, non-showy manner and the world at large might not be aware of what the Nine has done.

At an advanced psychological level, the Nine with a One wing finds great happiness and fulfilment in the work they do, empowering and teaching other people. They no longer feel the urge to withdraw and involve themselves in a meaningful way in the world. Their dreams become reality at last and others feel the full benefit of their self-actualized power.

In a not-so-healthy state, the Nine with the One wing will tend to withdraw in a typical Nine way and become more judgmental of the self and others in a typical One way. They might retreat into a comfortable fantasy world and are inevitably disappointed when their real life interactions do not live up to their fantasies.

When bad goes to worse, they become more upset with the discrepancies between their inner fantasy world and outside reality. They cope with this scenario by isolating themselves. Worst case scenario, they might even become psychotic, where they're barely present in a body that gradually goes to rack and ruin.

It would be quite typical for a Peacemaker with a One wing to find work that allows them to use their mind but not necessarily in a very exacting way. Examples might be astrologers, puppeteers and dressmakers.

The Type Nine with an Eight wing (9W8)

These people are the salt of the earth. The Peacemaker with an Eight wing may come across as a little rough-around-the-edges, but cuddly all the same, rather like an over-sized, clumsy puppy, eager for happiness. The inclination is towards gentleness and a lack of sophistication. The Eight will lend the Nine a tad more impulsiveness and forcefulness than they would normally have, but they will back down in the face of too much resistance. The Nine with the Eight wing is not overly eager to rise to every challenge either.

When a Nine with an Eight wing begins to self-actualize, he or she will use their energy and expansiveness to pull themselves out of passivity. They will then become generous, powerful and benevolent.

When fully actualized, the Peacemaker is a truly uplifting presence in the world. They are generous, humble and genuinely good. Just being in their sphere of influence is inspiring. They don't do anything, as such. They are just their wonderful selves.

But it's not all rainbows and unicorns! In a state of stress, the Nine with an Eight wing may be paranoid and become almost hermit like in his or her existence. They will be lazy and mistrustful.

At their absolute lowest level, avoidance becomes paramount as the 9W8 spurns all and any human interaction. It is a kind of semi-comatose state and the paranoid persuasions become worse.

In terms of physical appearance, the Nine with an Eight wing is often big and frequently strong. They will seldom be seen in flashy clothing and will strive for normality.

Advice for The Peacemaker

1. Body awareness is very important for the Nine. Exercise will help hugely here. It will allow you to discharge aggression and teach you to concentrate and focus your attention. You will become more aware of your feelings and benefit in terms of self-discipline.

2. Repressed anger causes damage, both to your physical and emotional health. Everybody has negative emotions, including you. When you fail to acknowledge this, you can disturb the harmony you so crave in your relationships. It is far healthier for you to be honest about your feelings - both with yourself and with loved ones - and get issues out in the open, fully aired!

3. You find it deeply difficult to examine pain. But looking honestly at why a relationship has gone wrong, and even worse, admitting to possibly contributing to this problem, is necessary, both for your peace of mind and for ensuring that such a situation does not repeat itself. This is how genuine relationships are created.

4. If it is possible to be *too* nice, then you as a Type Nine are arguably the most likely type on the Enneagram to fall into this trap. Not only is it bad for your own sake to be constantly acquiescing to other people's needs, especially with loved ones, it is also bad for the other person and for the relationship as a whole. Keeping the peace can sometimes come at a high price. You have to be yourself to have a successful and genuine relationship. Only when you are completely honest about your own needs can you be truly there for the other person.

5. Daydreaming is not a bad past time per se. However, when overused as a means of tuning out of the world around you, this is not so healthy. You should try to engage with people and participate meaningfully in society.

Conclusion

So, we come to the end of this book. Have you read it all? Or have you just skipped to your type or the type you *think* you are? Either way is absolutely fine. This book can be taken as a whole or dipped in and out of, as the reader so desires. The approach you take might depend on your type! A meticulous One may peruse each sentence thoroughly from start to finish, whereas an impulsive Seven, might just skip to the "good bits"! It really doesn't matter, as this book is written for each and every type on the Enneagram.

The aim of this book is to give you a thorough understanding of the Enneagram - the theory behind it, its origins, how it works and how it can work for you. You might be guided by what your friends and loved ones have commented about you and your personality over the years or better still, you may be guided by your own self-knowledge. Best of all, you might be led by your own internal guidance system. Whatever the case, this book has the capacity to add to your self-knowledge and your self-awareness. It is up to you to take it on board and to apply it to your own life. Remember, knowledge is power! Not over others but over the self. Self-mastery is key and knowing yourself is of the utmost importance. Applying this knowledge is gold!

We have covered a lot in the preceding chapters. In the introduction, we learned the origins of the word 'enneagram' and the names of the pioneers in the field, devising the methodology and developing the theory into the Enneagram we know today. Of course, many others who were not named throughout these pages have also made important contributions.

The Enneagram is a complex and useful blend of the wisdom of our predecessors and the insights of modern psychology. As such, it can lend a deep understanding of the self, augmenting what we have already learned throughout our life experiences. It can be used for personal growth, for adding spiritual depth, for working out with whom we are compatible and for understanding our close friends and family members in more depth. We can use it in the area of our careers also. So that is why our boss behaves the way he does! Or why that co-worker can sometimes appear so odd! With insight and understanding comes compassion and hopefully, less conflict too.

This book will help you to understand the positives and negatives of each type, both your own and that of all the people around you. Better understanding all round.

Chapter One taught us about the symbol which represents the Enneagram, how it is constructed out of three separate shapes brought together to make one whole. We have the circle, representing the wholeness of life, the triangle, representing the 'magic' number three and the hexad, an unusual, irregular shape, borrowed from the Sufi tradition, representing the law of seven and the law of octaves.

Within the shape are placed the numbers One to Nine which we now know as the nine Types of the Enneagram and the lines on the symbol demonstrate the connections between the different types.

We have further learned that the Enneagram is not a blunt instrument but an exact tool to be wielded subtly. Accordingly, each person is not made of entirely one personality type. The Enneagram gives you wings! You discover your wing by looking at the numbers on either side of yours and ascertaining for yourself which one most closely aligns with you and your unique character.

We then discovered that the Enneagram and its symbol is structured into three separate triads and that each triad holds a different emotion: One, Eight and Nine are rulers of instinct, Two, Three and Four are in the feeling center, and Five, Six and Seven are in the thinking triad.

Enneagram

You will have noticed how each and every chapter begins with a handy check list, allowing you, the reader, to work out as quickly as possible exactly who you are or to point you in the right direction at least. Think of these check lists as sign posts, pointing you towards your correct destination.

You will have learned that when it comes to the Enneagram, it is more likely to be nature rather than nurture which hold the key. A Type appears to be born rather than made and despite the many and varied changes that happen in our lives, our basic type will remain unchanged, as a constant that can be relied upon. And fundamentally, no type is the 'best' type. We can all strive to be the most wonderful version of ourselves.

Along our journey of discovery about The Enneagram, we also found out about the levels. In other words, that there are three basic levels of development in this system: healthy, average or neutral and unhealthy. Therefore, a healthy One, for example, can look like a totally different creature, and indeed type, than an unhealthy One. Each level is, in turn, divided into the sub-levels, in descending or ascending orders, depending on what way you look at it! Yet another example of the subtlety of the Enneagram. Knowing simply which type you are is not knowing the entire story.

It might be helpful to give you a brief summary of the nine different types and the basic characteristics of each one. So, in numerical order and not in order of importance, I give you the Enneagram:

1. Type One is known as the Reformer or the Perfectionist and, as always, these names reveal a great deal. The Reformer values principles and integrity above all and his or her primary motivation is to be both right and good. They strive for perfection at all times and try to maintain self-control. Quality is of utmost importance and the One will appreciate structure and standards.

Enneagram

The Reformer or Perfectionist has many sterling qualities to offer, such as dignity, discernment, tolerance, serenity and acceptance. Their shadow sides, however, mean that they can be acutely critical of themselves and others, pedantic, uncompromising and judgemental.

2. Type Two is the Helper. Their modus operandi is to be appreciated and liked. They value their relationships above all else and will be generous, kind and self-sacrificing towards this end. They would dearly love to make the world a better place and genuinely try to do this, giving loving attention and support to those they care about. They shine when it comes to being unconditionally supportive. They are also humble beings, who are capable of practicing healthy self-care. On the not-so-plus side, they might be manipulative and flattering in their mode of giving as they strive to get back what they have given.

3. The Achiever, which is Type Three, wants to be the best! Their priorities include results, efficiency, image and recognition. They are capable of being flexible in order to achieve their goals. Anything for success! At his or her best, The Achiever offers those around them hope and integrity. They are also principled, hard working and receptive. At the worst, they can come across as inconstant and self-important. This is because their sense of self is erroneously based on what they do instead of who they are.

4. Type Four, the Individualist, is driven by his or her intense need to express authenticity and uniqueness. Individualism, as the name suggests, is highly valued, as are self-expression, feelings and purpose. They are romantic souls and beauty will be very important to them, as is meaning. The best of the Four is authenticity and equanimity, sensitivity and contentment. The shadow side of the Individualist shows someone who is melancholic, temperamental and believes themselves to be misunderstood.

5. Type Five, the Investigator, is deeply motivated to know and to understand. They love to make sense of the world around them, valuing knowledge and objectivity. Privacy and independence are priorities for this type and at their best, they are mindful and even visionary. But the darker Five is arrogant, stingy and disconnected from their emotions.

6. Type Six, the Loyalists, are very big on belonging and security and their constant drive is to be safe and well-prepared. As the name implies, they value loyalty and trust and they are responsible sorts. The healthy Six is brave and devoted and possesses a sense of inner knowing. When unhealthy, they can be doubting, suspicious or anxious and they may fear letting down their defenses and worry to an excessive level.

7. Type Seven, or the Enthusiast wants to experience all and everything that life has to offer, while avoiding pain in the process. They value freedom and they are optimistic and inspired. Life is a big adventure for the Enthusiast with many opportunities along the way to play and be spontaneous. At their best they are serene and content. At their worst, they can be easily distracted, unfocused, impulsive and uncommitted.

8. Type Eight, the Challenger, only likes to act from a place of strength and dislikes displaying their weaknesses. Control is very important to them and they desire to have an impact in their own direct way. They do love a challenge and will protect those that they perceive to be more vulnerable than themselves. At a healthy level, they are caring, strong and approachable. When unhealthy, they can be aggressive and domineering.

9. Type Nine, or the Peacemaker, wants nothing more than to be in harmony with the world. They place great importance on being

accommodating and accepting. They love peace and stability while hating conflict. At their best, they are vibrant and self-aware. At their worst, they can be stubborn and inclined to procrastinate.

So I hope that you have found the information provided in this book and the way in which it has been presented to be of use to you. The basics have been covered and expanded upon, and a comprehensive and hopefully engaging guide has been provided. I hope that you have managed to identify your personality type and gain self-knowledge in the process. You should now have all the tools at your disposal.

I wish you the very best of luck on your Enneagram journey and indeed, on your journey throughout life. If there is one thing I would love for you to take away from this book, it is this: that there is no such thing as a good type or a bad type. Each personality type encompasses all aspects and no one type is better than another. As we examine our type and the different levels, my hope for all of us is that we strive for the pinnacle of health and maturity, knowing we are meant for better.

www.ingramcontent.com/pod-product-compliance
Lightning Source LLC
Chambersburg PA
CBHW031109080526
44587CB00011B/889